DEDICATION

To my wife, Shirley, and my two children, Lynne Nowaczek
and Bryan Meck. All three have been extremely supportive
and encouraging in my thirty years of writing.

BOOKS BY CHARLES R. MECK

The Hatches Made Simple
Pennsylvania Trout Streams and Their Hatches
Arizona Trout Streams and Their Hatches (with John Rohmer)
Mid-Atlantic Trout Streams and Their Hatches
How to Catch More Trout
Meeting and Fishing the Hatches
Fishing Small Streams with a Fly Rod
101 Innovative Fly-Tying Techniques

101 Innovative Fly-Tying Techniques

How to Tie Flies Quickly, Easily, and Professionally

CHARLES R. MECK

THE LYONS PRESS
Guilford, Connecticut
An imprint of The Globe Pequot Press

Printed in the United States of America

10 9 8 7 6 5 4 3 2 1

Library of Congress Cataloging-in-Publication Data

Meck, Charles R.
  101 innovative fly-tying techiques : how to tie flies quickly,
 easily, and professionally / by Charles R. Meck.
      p. cm.
   ISBN 1-58574-751-3 (hc : alk. paper)
  1. Fly tying. 2. Flies, Artificial. I. Title: One hundred one
 innovative fly-tying techiques. II. Title.
   SH451 .M435 2002
   688.7'9124—dc21
                                              2002014801

Contents

Acknowledgments

Thirty years ago I had an idea: I wanted to sell a box of flies that had an overlay of the hatches that these patterns matched and the approximate date that the hatches appeared. I searched for some local fly tiers to tie many of the patterns. I hunted for more than a year and found very few good tiers. I finally gave up on the idea because of the paucity of tiers. That was thirty years ago. How times have changed since then! Now I find excellent fly tiers in every small town I visit.

Yes, fly tying has changed dramatically. The entire industry is exploding with new materials and tying methods because of the increasing number of tiers. I was fortunate when working on this book to have the help of some really outstanding tiers. They came up with a lot of the innovative techniques. Some of these great tiers include Mike O'Brien, editor of the *Mid Atlantic Fly Fishing Guide;* Kurt Thomas, a guide out of Ridgway, Pennsylvania; Garry Hitterman, a professional fly tier from Casa Grande, Arizona; and Chip Hidinger of Mesa, Arizona, one of those new, really knowledgeable fly tiers. Without their help I could never have completed this book.

Introduction

I have tied flies for more than fifty years, but I'm a lazy tier. I take many shortcuts to cut down on the time it takes to tie a fly. For years I've tied flies in workshops and classes at fly-fishing shows in Pennsylvania, New Jersey, Colorado, Arizona, and New Mexico. In those many years of fly tying I've learned a lot of time-saving techniques—many that I've gained from other anglers, and some I've developed myself.

In my classes I've had anglers come up to me and say they learned a lot of innovative techniques while watching me. These techniques make tying time shorter and the whole process easier and much more effective. Some of the techniques even strengthen patterns and make them more durable.

I also believe in the phrase Keep It Simple, Stupid (KISS). Most of the patterns I tie are not complicated. You won't find any woven bodies here, and you won't find any complicated classic salmon patterns. What you will find are a lot of easy-to-tie, highly productive flies.

In addition to fly-tying techniques, I'll show you the actual descriptions for tying forty-six highly productive patterns. Have you seen a beadhead Glo Bug—or a Deer-Head Caddis? Have you ever tied a Twisted Caddis or Twisted Dun? What about the recipe for a Strike

Indicator? You'll find the tying directions for all of these and many more in this book. In each chapter I'll tie a few patterns to show you some different tying techniques. Each time I use a new technique I'll italicize it in the tying directions in that chapter. Sections that are both italicized and boldfaced in the tying directions explain the reason for using the technique. At the beginning of each chapter you'll find a section entitled "Techniques You Will Learn in This Chapter." Here I list that chapter's share of the 101 innovative techniques incorporated in the book. You'll also find sections on fishing and tying the different patterns included in each chapter.

Many of the techniques I list in the following chapters will make your tying easier and quicker. You'll see different ways to whip-finish and half-hitch a fly, use a built-in hackle guard, and prevent beads from falling on the floor. Some of the techniques will strengthen the fly. For instance, I show you how to prevent slippery synthetic materials from sliding back over the body and give several tips for holding wings in place. Still other suggestions make the patterns more lifelike.

Other techniques listed in the upcoming chapters are not really techniques at all but rather methods for using relatively new or unknown materials. Organza makes fantastic spinner wings; the material is lifelike and easy to work with. We'll look at this material when we tie spentwing patterns in Chapter 6. You'll also see how to use Flex Foam for body material when I tie the Twisted Brown Drake in Chapter 8.

Finally, some methods I suggest protect specific parts of the fly. Have you ever had a bead discolor after using it for a period of time? I prevent this by placing some nail polish or epoxy on the bead. You'll see this mentioned when I tie the Golden Shiner in Chapter 9.

Not much in fly tying is really new. Yes, some effective new materials have come on the scene the past two decades. Z-lon, poly, Antron, and dozens of others help to produce effective patterns. But a fly-tying technique I consider new might have been created by another tier years ago. I thought I created something different when I first tied the Twisted

Dun with side markings. After I wrote about that tying procedure in the *Mid Atlantic Fly Fishing Guide,* I received a note from one of the editors of the magazine, Mike O'Brien. Mike told me that he had used the twist technique to make poly bodies for almost two decades—so much for an innovative idea. Every time I discuss a new tying technique with George Harvey, he invariably says that he used that same technique fifty years ago. So, what is new to me might not be to you. With millions of fly tiers—and the number continues to grow—it's unlikely that what I think is new actually is.

What is the correct way to tie a pattern? I say there is no one correct way—just the one that suits you best and the one with which you feel most comfortable. Some tiers would have you believe that their way is the correct and only way to tie a fly. On the other hand, I say the way with which you feel most at ease is the best way to tie a fly. So, if these recommendations fit your tying persona, then use them.

How do I separate the chapters in this book? I've divided them according to the type of fly tied. You will see some of the basics in Chapter 1. Here you'll learn about new techniques like making the whip-finish and half-hitch with ease.

Chapter 2 looks at some methods for tying nymphs and emergers. It also deals with innovative techniques for tying legs on these flies. The legs for a Hendrickson Emerger are a great example. You'll tie the Hendrickson Emerger, Pheasant-Tail Nymph, Quigley Wiggler, Swimming Ephemera Nymph, and March Brown Nymph. The Quigley Wiggler is an excellent pattern to get that movement you want in some of the larger emerging nymphs. Chapter 2 describes and illustrates nineteen innovative techniques.

Wet flies are probably the easiest of the patterns to tie, yet anglers often overlook them. In Chapter 3 I'll tie important new wet flies such as the Sunken Ant, Zebra Midge, and a weighted beadhead Glo Bug. Tying and using the Zebra Midge is worth the price of this book. Along with the patterns in Chapter 3 you'll see nine innovative techniques for tying some basic wet flies.

Terrestrials are an important part of any angler's arsenal. An ant, beetle, or cricket pattern saved many of my midsummer fishing trips. Chapter 4 shows some neat tricks to use when you're tying terrestrial patterns. Some of these tying tricks will help you follow the pattern better on streams with a heavy canopy. These techniques will make terrestrial patterns like the Sunken Ant, Winged Ant, and Chernobyl Cricket easier to tie and much more durable. I suggest seven techniques to tie these patterns.

Chapter 5 examines conventional dry flies and some innovative methods for tying them. Have you ever tied on a body of tinsel or one of the new synthetics and had the material slip back over the bend of the hook after catching one trout? I'll show you how to prevent that type of body material from slipping back over the bend, and give you many other ideas for tying bodies and wings. For making tails, I'll show you an easy method of making certain the hackle barbules are of equal length and the correct size for the pattern. You'll also see some new—and some not-so-new—materials for making tails. Chapter 5 describes fourteen innovative methods and techniques through a series of patterns like the Patriot, Strike Indicator, Upright Spinner, and Hybrid.

What about spinners or spentwing patterns? Are there some different methods for tying these flies? What happens when a spinner falls spent on the surface a mile upstream from where you are fishing? Probably the dead adult has sunk beneath the surface by the time it reaches the area you are fishing. Trout feed on these. Don't overlook the importance of sunken spinners. You'll find directions for tying the Weighted Trico, Red Quill Spinner, Twisted Coffin Fly, and others—plus eleven innovative techniques for tying them—in Chapter 6.

Anglers match caddisfly and stonefly hatches with flies they call "down-wings." These patterns are extremely important as a part of the cache of the fly fisher. Chapter 7 examines these adults with wings folded back over their bodies and gives eleven techniques for tying these highly productive patterns. Flies like the Deer-Head Caddis, Twisted

Tan Caddis, Kurt's Caddis, Simple Salmon, Black Caddis, and Fluttering Green Caddis will change the way you fish forever.

Chapter 8 looks at a different type of dry fly—the parachute. Did you know that there's an easy way to prevent hackle from going up and over the wing (post) of a parachute dry fly? And how can you prevent the post from moving forward? You'll learn fifteen techniques by tying parachute patterns such as the Slate Drake, Vernille-bodied Little Blue-Winged Olive, Blue Quill, and Twisted Brown Drake.

What about tying streamers and bucktails? In Chapter 9, I look at old favorites like the Lady Ghost and Green Weenie, and some relatively new patterns like the Sparkle-Head Streamer and Golden Shiner. You'll also see thirteen techniques designed to help you tie more effective patterns.

Finally, in Chapter 10, you'll tie some relatively new patterns like the Stimulator. These awkward-looking flies often catch trout when nothing else does—especially when matching one of the large caddisfly, stonefly, or drake hatches. The Laid Back Hex is an important part of this chapter. You'll learn two new tying procedures in Chapter 10.

That's it! That's 101 innovative techniques in ten chapters. Now, sit back, enjoy, tie, and use the *101 Innovative Fly-Tying Techniques*.

1

The Basics

SOME DIFFERENT TYING TECHNIQUES

I've been tying flies since 1949. George Harvey was my first teacher at a Junior Conservation Camp conducted by Penn State University. I classify myself as a lazy tier, and if I find productive shortcuts I eagerly use them. There are dozens of methods I use in fly tying that I have found extremely effective. The first is a method for tying wings on a dry fly. A second technique has a duel purpose: It prevents the body from moving back over the tail, and also prevents the hackle on a parachute-style fly from moving up over the post. Another gimmick I use is useful with beads. These are just a few of the techniques I've adopted over the years and that I will share with you in the following pages.

Remember, many tiers are already using many if not most of these methods—I'm just spreading the word.

Dividing Dry-Fly Wings (Chapter 5—Patriot)

Plenty of fly tiers have trouble with dry-fly wings. Whether they're tied from deer hair, calf hair, or a duck flank feather, the method I use separates the wings quickly and holds them in position permanently. I use

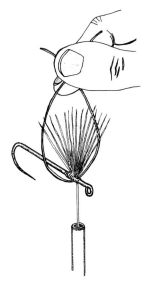

Dividing the Wings with a Harness
Step one: *Create-a-loop and cut the strand totally (both butt sections near the shank), place under the hook and behind (or you can do it from the front) the wing.*

this technique when tying the Patriot. Here's the simple method:

Tie in the white calf body hair on the shank about one-third of the way back from the hook eye. You want the wings to be as long as the hook shank. Make plenty of wraps over the butt section of the calf hair to firmly secure the wings to the shank. Lift the calf hair up and make about a dozen turns of thread just in front of the wings to make them stand erect. Next, tie in a six-inch piece of tying thread just behind the wings. Take that new piece of tying thread and divide the wings in half, going from the back to the front of the wing. Wrap the new thread completely around the left wing and back to the shank. Move the thread until you're satisfied with the

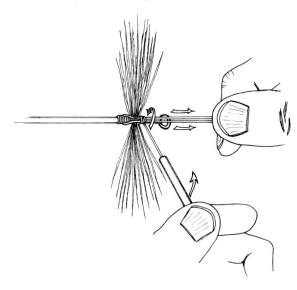

Step two: *Pull the two ends through the middle of the wings from the back to the front (or front to back). Once you get the wings to the desired spread tie down the harness. Cut off remaining strands.*

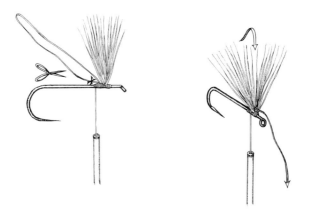

Dividing Wings and Forming a Figure-Eight with a Single Strand of Thread
Step one: *Create-a-loop and cut off one end at the shank of the hook.*
Step two: *Take the single strand of thread (we will call this the loose thread) and bring it through the middle of the hair wing.*

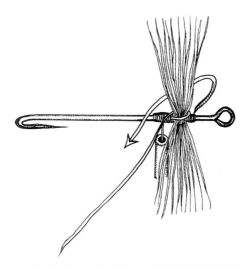

Step three: *Continue with the loose thread around the left half of the wing.*

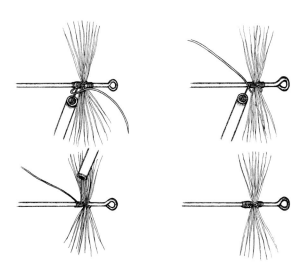

Step four: *Lock the loose thread behind the wing with the thread that is still attached to the bobbin and take the remaining thread through the middle.*
Step five: *Take the loose thread completely around the right wing.*
Step six: *Tie off the loose thread behind the wing so the final product looks like* **Step seven.**

wing placement. You might have to make more than one complete turn on unmanageable wings. Then make a couple of turns with your regular tying thread over the loose piece of thread to secure the short piece. Next, use the added tying thread and wrap it around the right wing. Follow the same procedure as with the left wing. This thread first divides the wing in half—then it pulls back and keeps the wings separated. This technique is quick, easy, and simple.

Preventing Body Material from Moving Back over the Tail (Leave-a-strand) (Chapter 5—Patriot)

If you use Krystal Flash or other synthetics as body material, you'll find that they often move back over the bend of the hook and mess up the fly. There's an easy tying method to prevent the material from moving back over the tail and into the bend of the hook. Here's how you do it when tying the Patriot. Tie in five 6-inch pieces of smolt blue Krystal

Leave-a-strand. *Follow the directions for tying the Patriot. When you tie in the body, tie in five strands of smolt blue Krystal Flash. Leave one of the strands behind. Wind the other four strands around the shank and halfway up to the eye. Tie in the four with the red tying thread.*

Take the lone strand left at the bend and pull it over top of the four wound strands.

Tie in this fifth strand where you tied in the others.

Flash just in front of the tail. Keep one of these pieces to the rear and wind the other four about halfway up the shank. Tie them in with the red tying thread. Now pull the fifth piece of Krystal Flash up over the body and tie it where you just tied the others in. This method prevents the body from slipping back.

Using Beads (Chapter 2—Pheasant-Tail Nymph)

When you use beads, do you lose a lot of them on the floor? Try dipping

Place beads on a wax tube so they don't fall on the floor.

a tube of tying wax into a bag of beads. Keep the beads on the wax until you're ready to use them. Position the beads so the hook goes through the smaller opening first. You'll find that few if any fall onto the floor.

Splitting the tail. *Take a six-inch piece of thread. You can use the create-a-loop method. Cut off both ends and take the loop of that thread under the shank and over the point of the hook.*

Try to divide the barbules into three equal pieces. Bring the loose ends of the thread through the tails from the rear toward the eye.

Make a couple of turns with the tying thread around the loose end of the looped thread, and then pull it tight to spread the tail. Make a few wraps with the tying thread to secure.

Spreading the Hackle Fibers for the Tail (Chapter 6—Red Quill Spinner)

I've always had difficulty spreading out hackle tail fibers. Why worry about that? I recently did an experiment during a Trico spinner fall. I used one pattern where the tail fibers were all clumped together and a second Trico pattern where the tails were spread out. Guess what? I caught considerably more trout on the pattern with the spread tail. It was enough to change my thinking on a spread versus clumped tail.

But to get the tail I wanted took three or four steps, and I will tell you many times in this book that I'm a lazy tier. I came up with two other solutions—the one that I prefer more I'll describe briefly here. Make a harness with a six-inch piece of tying thread. Double the loose piece of tying thread, and place the loop down and over the point of the hook. Bring the loop up to the tail. Now bring the two ends of the thread so they split the tail fibers in approximately three equal parts. Pull on the ends of the thread until you get the desired spread and tie in front of the tail. Using this technique will give you a great splayed tail.

Create-a-loop (Chapter 2—March Brown Nymph)

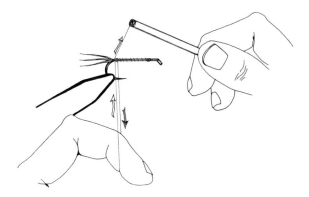

Create-a-loop
Step one: *Make a loop with the tying thread around your finger. Over-wrap the base of the loop three times with the tying thread.*

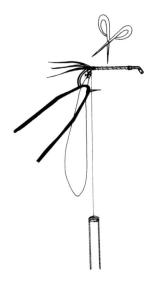

Step two: *Cut off one end of the loop at the shank. You should now have a single piece of thread.*

Often a tying recipe calls for a piece of tying thread tied in just in front of the tail. You'll often use that piece of thread to rib the body. If you're like me you've probably cut off a piece of tying thread and tied that in at the bend with the tying thread still attached to the bobbin. There's a much easier, faster way to attach this loose piece of thread at the rear. Make a three-inch loop with the tying thread attached to the bobbin (I call this "create-a-loop"). Tie over the loop with several turns of tying thread. Leave the loop behind and now dub the body.

After you've finished dubbing the body, cut one end of the loop at the shank and rib the body with the loose tying thread. You'll use this method several times in the book beginning with the March Brown Nymph in Chapter 2. You can use it when you divide the wings and in many other processes.

A Simple Whip-Finish
(Chapter 2—Hendrickson Emerger)

For years I've seen fly tiers struggle with whip-finishing by hand and with a special whip-finishing tool. There's an easy method of whip-finishing and half-hitching without a special tool or working by hand. Take the thread still attached to the head of the fly. Put your short-nozzled bobbin on top of the thread and wind the thread around the bobbin three or four times. Take the nozzle of the bobbin up to the eye of the hook and slide the wound thread over the eye of the hook.

Use a short-nozzled bobbin like a Cross or S&M bobbin. If you don't have a bobbin, use the front half of an empty ballpoint pen. Wind

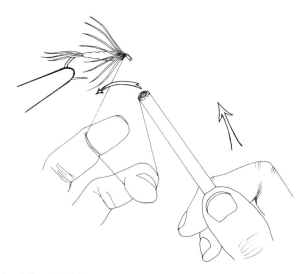

Whip-Finish with a Bobbin
Step one: *Move the bobbin over top of the thread that is coming from the fly.*

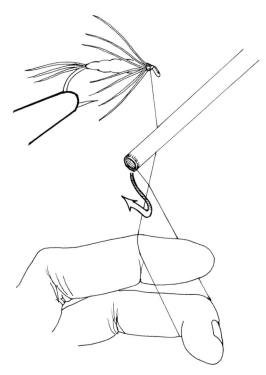

Step two: *Touch the bobbin to the thread so that you've created an X.*

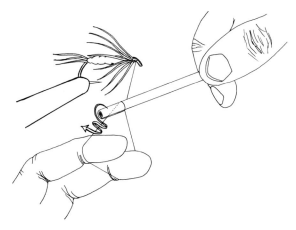

Step three: *Take the thread coming from the fly and wrap it around the nozzle three times until it resembles* **Step four.**

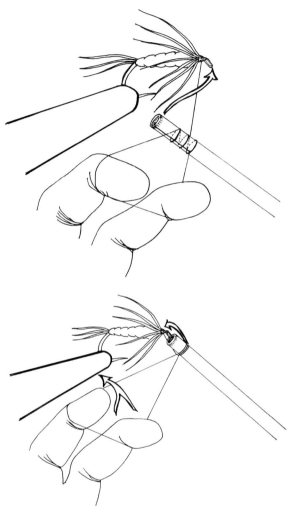

Step five: *Bring the nozzle to the eye of the hook and slide the thread wraps over the eye of the hook.*

the tying thread around the front part of the pen, slide the thread over the eye of the hook, and pull tight. George Harvey and Joe Humphreys have used this technique for half-hitching and whip-finishing for years—long before I did. It's really not a whip-finish in the true sense— it's a group of half-hitches—but it holds thread securely.

In addition to being used as a whip-finisher, the nozzle can also become a hackle guard. As you slip off the thread, it automatically pushes the hackle back (Chapter 5—Patriot).

Preventing Hackle from Climbing Up a Post. (Chapter 8—Slate Drake and the Little Blue-Winged Olive Dun)

Preventing hackle from climbing up a post. Tie in a three-inch piece of the tying thread with the post. You can do this with the create-a-loop method.

There are two possible solutions to hackle creeping up the post of a parachute dry fly. First, you can wind the hackle high on the post and make succeeding turns lower. But, if the hackle loosens for any reason, it will still slip off the post. Tie in a three-inch piece of thread with the post and wind the hackle around that thread and the post. Next, bring that piece of thread down over the hackle and tie off just behind the hook eye.

IS PERFECT ALWAYS BEST?

All of us strive to tie the best possible fly. We make certain that the wings are tied on the hook perfectly, and that the tail, hackle, and body are as close to the natural we're matching as possible. I've always been intrigued with that philosophy. But if you've studied hatches, then you already realize that when mayflies, stoneflies, and caddisflies emerge on the surface, often only the crippled or malformed can't take flight. Take a careful look at the next hatch you see and examine some of the insects that remain on the surface. Some have a wing missing, some are still attached to their nymphal shuck, and others have atrophied legs.

So, when you tie that next pattern, remember that the insects the trout often feed on are the cripples, deformed and not perfectly shaped. Why should your pattern be perfectly shaped? Shouldn't it copy that cripple?

PATTERNS TIED TO SHOW THE 101 TECHNIQUES

Rather than just read about these 101 techniques, I feel it is important for you to practice them. You'll do that by tying the forty-six patterns described in this book. I've included each of these patterns for a purpose; as you tie each pattern, you'll learn at least one of the 101 techniques. You'll find each new technique listed in italics. If I think the technique is extremely important, I've placed it in italics in several different tying exercises. Here are the patterns you'll tie. Remember, each has a purpose.

Chapter 2—Emergers and Nymphs

Hendrickson Emerger
Pheasant-Tail Nymph
Quigley Wiggler
March Brown Nymph
Swimming Ephemera Nymph

Chapter 3—Wet Flies

I'm Not Sure
Green Weenie
Glo Bug
Zebra Midge
March Brown
Bugskin Crayfish
Tungsten Black Caddis

Chapter 4—Terrestrials

Plastic Beetle
Elk Hop
Chernobyl Cricket
Sunken Cinnamon Ant
Winged Ant
Deerhair or Poly Ant

Chapter 5—Conventional Dry Flies

Patriot
Strike Indicator
Hybrid
Upright Spinner
Chocolate Dun

Chapter 6—Spentwings

Sulphur, Gray Drake, and Dark Brown Spinners
Weighted Female Trico Spinner
Twisted Green Drake Spinner
Twisted Coffin Fly Spinner
Red Quill Spinner

Chapter 7—Down-Wings

Black Caddis
Deer-Head Caddis
Fluttering Deer-Head Caddis
Twisted Caddis
Simple Salmon
Kurt's Caddis

Chapter 8—Parachutes

Slate Drake
Little Blue-Winged Olive Dun
Blue Quill
Twisted Brown Drake

Chapter 9—Streamers and Bucktails

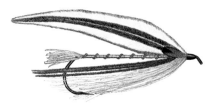

Bead-Head Woolly Bugger
Lady Ghost
Sparkle-Head Streamer
Golden Shiner

Chapter 10—Stimulator Type Patterns

Laid Back Hex
Convertible

A COMMON FLY-TYING LANGUAGE

Before we proceed, we need to develop a common language. Throughout this book I'll use various terms to describe the materials and tools we'll be using to tie a variety of great fish-catching flies. Here is a brief glossary of those terms. Study it now so you'll be ready when it comes time to tie the flies and practice the 101 techniques. And later, flip back to this chapter if you run across a word with which you are unfamiliar; there's a good chance you'll find it here.

I'm going to define the types of flies we will tie, the tools we will use, as well as several common fly-tying materials. There's also a hook chart which will help you find substitute hooks for those I list in the fly-pattern recipes. This is all good information you'll want to know.

The Fly

Wet Fly

A wet fly is a pattern that is fished underneath the surface. This pattern often copies the emerger and nymph of an aquatic insect. Fly tiers often use soft, absorbent materials and heavier hooks so these patterns sink.

Dry Fly

A dry fly is a pattern that is usually fished on the surface. It often copies an adult or sub-adult mayfly, stonefly, caddisfly, terrestrial, midge, or crane fly. Fly tiers use lighter materials and hooks, and stiffer hackle and hair for these.

Terrestrial

An insect that is usually found on land but is often blown or otherwise transported onto the surface of the stream. Terrestrials include, but are not limited to, ants, beetles, crickets, and grasshoppers.

Streamers and Bucktails

These flies are often designed to copy minnows and other baitfish, and are often made from hair and/or hackle.

Down-Wings

So called because the wings lie back over the body. These patterns often copy stoneflies and caddisflies.

Nymph

Nymphs are wet-fly patterns that are usually fished under the surface and often copy the larvae of mayflies and stoneflies. They are often built with weight, heavier hooks and absorbent materials.

Emerger

An emerger pattern is one that copies the stage between the nymph and dun of the mayfly and the pupal stage of the caddisfly. An emerger is a fly that copies the nymph changing into a dun.

Stimulator

These are down-wing patterns developed by Randall Kaufman that copy many stonefly and caddisfly patterns. These patterns can also be very effective with some of the large mayfly (drake) hatches.

Types of Dry Flies

Catskill Pattern

The typical conventional upright dry fly with hackle tied in front of and behind the usually divided upright wing. This type of fly often rides high.

Comparadun

A low-riding dry fly that usually has deer hair as the wing. The deer hair is tied in an arc and helps float the pattern, and it imitates the wings and the legs.

Parachute

A type of dry-fly pattern with one wing, called a post, and the hackle wound around that post. A parachute rides much lower in the water than the Catskill fly.

Parts of the Hook

Point

The sharp part of the hook used to penetrate the fish's mouth.

Barb

That part of the hook that is located near the point and is used to help keep the trout from getting off the hook. I get rid of that part before I tie by mashing the barb in the jaws of the vise.

Bend

The rounded part of the hook at the rear.

Shank

This is the long flat part of the hook between the bend and the eye. Some hooks have a short shank; some have a longer shank than normal.

Eye

The loop at the front of the hook used to connect to your tippet. If you have difficulty threading some of the eyes on smaller hooks, some manufacturers, like Orvis, now make hooks with larger eyes.

Parts of the Fly

Hackle

Feathers often found in wet and dry flies to copy the legs and tails, and sometimes the wings, of naturals. These are usually from the neck or saddle (back) of a hen or rooster. The softer hen fibers are often used for wings or the hackle of a wet fly. The saddle and neck hackle of a rooster are used for the legs and tails on a dry fly and for the wings on many streamer patterns.

Hackle quality has improved geometrically in the past few decades. I can still remember the hackle I bought from the Herter's catalog thirty years ago. Those imported necks had a lot to be desired. With the advent of Bucky Metz's necks, quality became a given. For my money you can't beat a Charlie Collins neck. Charlie operates out of Pine City, New York, and has quality necks at very reasonable prices.

Tails

These are hackle fibers that extend out over the bend of the hook. These barbules are often equal in length to the shank of the hook on a typical dry fly. Tails can be made from other materials like deer and elk hair and synthetics.

Tag

Usually made of tinsel or wire wrapped on the bend of the hook under the tail and behind the butt.

Butt
The butt is usually a couple of turns of a feather just in front of the tail.

Ribbing
A thread or wire that is spiral or "palmer" wrapped on the body.

Body
The body is that part of the fly that is tied on the shank of the hook. This is the main part of the fly.

Wings
Hackle or other material, natural or synthetic, that is tied in just behind the eye on the top of the hook. The wing can be upright (parachute), divided (Catskill), deer hair in a semicircle (Comparadun), or it can be in a down-wing fashion slanting back over the body as with a streamer, bucktail, or caddis or stonefly pattern.

Cheek
A cheek is a feather that is placed on the side of the streamer just behind the hook eye.

Shoulder
A shoulder is usually a feather that is placed behind the cheek and in front of the wing. This is most often found on streamer and salmon type patterns.

Throat
Often found in streamers and bucktails. The throat is found on the front bottom of the pattern.

Tools

Vise
The vise is the major tool in fly tying. It holds the hook in place so you can tie comfortably. As long as you're going to purchase a vise, you might as well get a good one. Get a rotary vise—one that you can twist and

turn with ease. Rotary vises make tying so much easier. You can rotate the vise to wind a hackle, to place a body material on a shank, or to do so many other techniques. Make certain the vise has a material clip to hold one material when you're using another one.

Bodkin

An ice-pick type of tool used to tease out and hold materials.

Bobbin

A device used to hold the tying thread. There are many types of bobbins. I prefer those with a shorter nozzle. One with a shorter nozzle can be used to form whip-finishes and half-hitches.

Whip-Finisher

A whip-finisher is a device to help you form a knot to hold the thread in place. The best way is to use the bobbin, the end of a pen, or make a whip-finish with your fingers.

Scissors

Scissors come in various sizes and shapes. Get a good one that cuts readily.

Hackle Pliers

A hackle pliers is a tool used to wrap the hackle around the hook and hold other materials to keep them from unwinding.

Material Clip

A material clip holds materials out of the way. It's especially useful when tying a complicated pattern with many different materials.

Special Materials

I'm a craft-store junkie. I can spend hours in a craft store looking for synthetics, feathers, and other items that I might be able to use in fly tying. I've found lots of useful items in these stores: beads, foam of all types, feathers, threads, yarns and other fabrics.

Beads

These rounded or cone-shaped, often metallic materials have two holes in them. Always place the smaller hole in the front and the larger hole at the back. If you have trouble getting beads over scud hooks, bend the hook. I've always been frustrated that one size bead will fit over one Size 16 hook and not over the same size hook of another brand.

Eyes

Eyes come painted and add weight and reality to some streamer patterns.

Synthetics

Within the past decade or two the real advances in fly tying have come with the introduction of new materials. Flashabou, Krystal Flash, poly, foam, and Polycelon (a rubberlike cylinder for terrestrials) have all come into play. Make certain you read Phil Camera's book on synthetics.

Head Cement

For more than twenty years I've used clear fingernail polish for head cement. I buy it in discount shops for fifty cents a bottle.

Hooks

Hooks vary considerably from manufacturer to manufacturer. Try placing the same bead on two Size 14 scud hooks and you'll see; it might fit one hook but not another. Here are some of the more important hooks for fly tying and their general uses.

Table 1. Some of the more common hooks and their purposes

HOOK TYPE AND NUMBER	WIRE	EYE	LENGTH	PURPOSE
		DRY FLY		
Daiichi 1170	1x Standard	Down	Standard	Standard dry fly
Daiichi 1180	1x Fine	Down	Standard	Small barb
Daiichi 1190	1x Fine	Down	Standard	Barbless
Daiichi 1310	1x Fine	Down	Short shank	Tricos and other small flies
Daiichi 1480	1x Fine	Straight	2x Short	Midges
Orvis 1523	2x Fine	Down	Standard	Extra-fine
Orvis 1877	1x Fine	Down	Standard	Traditional dry fly
Orvis 4864	1x Fine	Down, enlarged	Standard	Oversized down eye for people who have difficulty threading a dry fly
Mustad 94831	2x Fine	Down	2XL	Used for larger patterns like the Hex and Green Drake
Mustad 94833	3x Fine	Down	Standard	Very light hook for dry flies
Mustad 94840	1x Standard	Down	Standard	Standard dry fly
Mustad 94842	Standard	Turned-up	Standard	Dry fly, turned-up eye
Mustad 94845	Standard	Down	Standard	Barbless
TMC 100	1x Fine	Down	Standard	Wide gap
Fenwick DSE	1x Fine	Straight	Standard	Dry fly, mini barb

Table 1.   Some of the more common hooks and their purposes (continued)

		WET FLY		
HOOK TYPE AND NUMBER	**WIRE**	**EYE**	**LENGTH**	**PURPOSE**
Mustad 9671	1x Stout	Down	2XL	Long wet fly, Green Weenie
Mustad 9672	1x Stout	Down	3XL	Muddlers, I'm Not Sure
Mustad 3908	2x Stout	Down	Standard	Heavy wet fly
Mustad 3906	1x Stout	Down	Standard	Standard wet fly
Tiemco (TMC) 8526	1x Stout	Down	Standard	Standard wet fly
		NYMPH		
Daiichi 1273	1x Strong	Straight	3XL	Curved-shank nymph hook
Daiichi 1560	1x Stout	Down	1XL	Nymph
Mustad 3906B	1x Stout	Down	1XL	Standard nymph hook
Tiemco (TMC) 8527	1x Stout	Down	XL	Nymph
		EMERGING PUPA/SCUD/BEADHEAD		
Daiichi 1150	1x Stout	Up	1x Short	Beadheads, scuds, emerging pupae
Orvis J8891	1x Fine	Down	1x Short	Beadheads, scuds, emerging pupae

That's enough background material. Let's start tying and using the 101 techniques.

2

Emergers and Nymphs

8. How to provide a stronger body for certain nymphs (Pheasant-Tail Nymph, steps 4 and 5)

9. How to make a lifelike, wiggling nymph on several small hooks (Quigley Wiggler)

10. How to connect the parts of the Quigley Wiggler (Quigley Wiggler, step 7)

11. How to make interchangeable parts for the Quigley Wiggler or other large nymphs (Quigley Wiggler, steps 2 through 5)

12. How to add weight to one part of the Quigley Wiggler to enhance its movement (Quigley Wiggler, step 6)

13. How to use wool or angora yarn as a darker back for nymphs (March Brown Nymph, step 3)

14. How to tie in a piece of tying thread for ribbing the body quickly and easily (create-a-loop) (March Brown Nymph, step 2)

15. How to rib both the back and the belly of a nymph at the same time (March Brown Nymph, step 3)

16. How to make a few strands of marabou look like the body and tail of a nymph (Swimming Ephemera Nymph, step 4)

17. How to use an aftershaft feather to imitate the gills of a nymph (Swimming Ephemera Nymph, step 6)

18. An easy way to place a bead on a hook without losing the bead. (Pheasant-Tail Nymph, step 1)

19. How to tie in two quill sections for a larger wing pad (March Brown Nymph, step 4)

Until a decade or two ago, anglers seldom heard the word "emerger" mentioned. In more recent years, the term and the patterns that copy it have become extremely important. All of us now realize that this phase of the life cycle of many aquatic insects encourages trout to feed voraciously. We all know that a nymph is the underwater stage or larva of a stonefly or mayfly. But what is an emerger, dun, or spinner? It's important that we examine the life cycle of a typical mayfly to understand the importance of each phase.

Although there are numerous exceptions, most mayfly species live underwater for about 360 days as nymphs (and eggs). The green drake nymph lives in a burrow for almost two years. As the nymph feeds and grows, it regularly sheds its skin (or *exoskeleton*) and develops a new one. Some species, depending on their size and the length of time they live as nymphs, go through five or more of these transformations (called *instars*) as they grow.

A year after the eggs are fertilized, the nymph begins to move toward the surface. At or near the water's surface, the nymph (now called an *emerger*) splits its skin dorsally and appears on the surface as a mayfly *dun* (or *subimago*), an immature, non-mating adult. There are exceptions, however, like *Epeorus*. This group emerges on or near the bottom. The process of changing from an underwater insect to an air-breathing one often takes time. The emerger stage, the transformation from a nymph to a dun, is the most vulnerable time in the life cycle of the mayfly (the process of the spinner falling spent on the surface is equally important, but in this stage they have less food value). Trout sense that this is one of the most defenseless stages in the entire life cycle and readily feed on nymphs that are changing into duns. The air-breathing mayfly dun rests on the water for a split second to several minutes (depending on the species and the weather) before flying away. Abnormally cold weather, especially in the spring and fall, delays or prevents the dun from taking flight. Overcast, drizzly conditions will often slow duns from taking off even in midsummer.

If and when the dun escapes, it flies toward a branch to rest. On extremely cold, miserable days, many duns struggle to reach rocks or debris on the shoreline and rest there. In a couple of hours to a day or more, the dun again goes through a change, loses its outer skin (*pellicle*), and becomes a *spinner* (also called an adult or *imago*) with glassy, clear wings. The spinner is a mating adult. Often, in the evening, male spinners form a swarm over or near the water, waiting for females to join them. When the females enter the swarm, the males impregnate them and the females move toward the water's surface and deposit their fertilized eggs. Mayflies live out of the water usually less than five days. Thus the name for the order of insects that contains the mayflies is Ephemeroptera, which comes from the Greek word for "short-lived."

This is a very generalized description and there are many exceptions. For example, some mayflies, such as the female white mayfly *(Ephoron), never* change into spinners but mate as duns. A few species remain as nymphs for two years (some *Ephemera* species) and many life cycles last only a few months (some *Baetis, Isonychia, Tricorythodes, and Callibaetis).* This latter type, with multiple broods, may appear many times a year.

When the term *hatch* is used in this book, it usually refers to duns emerging on the surface. When the nymph splits its pellicle or skin near the surface and changes into a dun, it is referred to as an *emerger. Spinner fall* is that time when females return to the water to deposit eggs and fall onto the surface, spent, or with wings outstretched. *Natural* refers to the nymph, dun, or spinner of a species. If you want more information on the life cycle of aquatic insects read *The Hatches Made Simple.*

FISHING EMERGERS AND NYMPHS

I hate fishing nymphs. I consider myself a poor nymph fisherman. That's why I usually fish these important underwater patterns with a strike indicator. Depth can be important when fishing nymphs. In cold weather and high-water conditions, fish the pattern close to or on the bottom. As the season progresses, and especially when you're fishing a hatch, try fishing the nymph closer to the surface. I most often fish emergers just under the surface.

Are emergers an important part of a trout's diet? Look at a study that Don Baylor, an entomologist of note, conducted during a sulphur hatch. Don extracted the stomach contents of several trout. He found that thirty-six of thirty-eight insects eaten were emergers. Are emergers important? You bet they are!

The emerger pattern is an effective one to use. Anglers often confuse a rise to the emerger as a rise to a dun. More often than not, trout are taking emergers just under the surface when we assume that they're taking duns.

Just how much of a fish-catcher are emerger patterns? Look at an old study that Paul Needham conducted more than fifty years ago in his book *Trout Streams.* That study is still valid today. Needham found that during June, July, and August, more than 70 percent of what trout eat is classified as mayflies. Of that amount, more than three-quarters are aquatic phases—nymphs and emergers—and less than 30 percent are adults. What does this tell the fly fisher? Using wet flies to copy nymphs and emergers is much more effective than using dry flies to copy duns and spinners.

Nymphs should most often be fished on or near the bottom, especially when there's no hatch or you experience cool weather or high water. When I get no strikes with a wet fly or nymph, more often than not it's because I'm not getting the pattern close enough to the bottom. In *How to Catch More Trout,* I said that one of the most important aspects is to fish the pattern where the trout are—that is, get the fly at the correct depth. With nymphs that often means fishing on or near the bottom.

Recently I watched Jeff Blood of western Pennsylvania fish a local stream in high water. Jeff is possibly the best high-stick-nymphing angler I have ever seen. While six of us had difficulty picking up a trout or two, Jeff easily caught at least a dozen on a Sulphur nymph. His secret? Jeff fished the nymph on the bottom. Sure he got hung up quite a bit, but he also caught trout.

TYING EMERGERS AND NYMPHS

Not all emergers should be tied in the same manner. The emerger is really a series of transitions from the nymph to the dun. As such, fly tiers should make some patterns with Krystal Flash or another bright, synthetic material to imitate an air bubble as the nymph pushes out its wing pad. On other patterns, add a piece of poly to imitate the wing coming out of the nymph's wing pad. On a third fly, you might tie the front half of the body to copy the dun and the back half to copy the nymph. On yet another fly, attach a piece of Z-lon to the tail of the dun pattern. Match the color of the nymph with the Z-lon. For instance, with the Sulphur and Pale Morning Dun, add a piece of dark brown Z-lon.

We usually tie nymphs in one size. For example, most of us tie a March Brown Nymph in a Size 12. However, depending on the time of year, a Size 14 or 16 might be more appropriate. If you're copying the March brown nymph, you might want to use a Size 16 in March and a Size 14 in April.

If you've ever examined the belly of a nymph you know that it is often much lighter than the back. Call it protective coloration, but most nymphs exhibit this two-tone color. You can achieve this effect when tying in two general ways (I'm certain that some of you have come up with other methods). First, you can tie an intricate woven body that might take an hour to make, or you can follow the method I use in tying the March Brown Nymph later in this chapter. This procedure takes only a few minutes.

Have you ever watched a nymph actually emerge into a dun? The process is often protracted and the nymph wiggles markedly while moving to the surface. I've watched green drakes (*Ephemera guttulata* and *Hexagenia rigida*) struggle to change into air-breathing insects. The struggle is violent and sometimes prolonged. The Quigley Wiggler copies this movement. We'll tie this pattern later in this chapter.

THE HENDRICKSON EMERGER

I've said many times that I'm a lazy fly tier. When I find an effective pattern that's easy to tie, I use it. Those are my two criteria—the pattern should be relatively easy to tie, and it should be productive. One pattern that meets these two criteria is the Hendrickson Emerger. It is definitely a productive pattern and is exceptionally easy to tie.

I found this tying method while fishing the Cache la Poudre River in Colorado. A fly fisher on that river handed me a pattern he called the Baetis Emerger. I did well with it, and also realized that it could be tied to match other hatches. I tied up some Hendrickson Emergers following the same procedure and tested them on streams across Pennsylvania, New Jersey, and New York on early-season trips. I hit a great hatch of hendricksons on the upper end of the South Branch of the Raritan River in New Jersey. I tied the emerger pattern behind a Hendrickson dry fly and fished them in tandem. I tied the emerger pattern a foot and a half behind the dry fly so it sank just beneath the surface. In one riffle in the early afternoon, thousands of hendrickson naturals rode the surface. Even though the water temperature that day didn't rise above 52 degrees Fahrenheit, more than a dozen trout fed in front of me during the hatch. I cast the tandem combo to the top of the riffle and caught ten of those trout—eight took the emerger pattern.

So the Hendrickson Emerger is an effective pattern, but is it easy to tie? You bet it is! The pattern has three parts to it—a tail, a body, and some long hackle that makes the wing pad and legs. I most often use a nymph hook to tie the fly so it sinks just beneath the surface. If you fish the pattern in the tandem rig behind a dry fly, you might want to add a few wraps of .010-inch lead wire to the body to keep the pattern just beneath the surface.

If you look closely at a natural hendrickson nymph, you'll see an almost black body with a light brown tail, brown legs, and black wing pad. To get the needed color scheme, use a furnace hackle for the combination wing pad and legs. The furnace hackle has a black center and brown edge.

Don't forget to dub the thorax area of the fly more heavily than the rear to give the appearance that the nymph is ready to emerge. It will take tying a fly or two to get the approximate length for the legs. If the legs are too long on the first few patterns, just cut off the excess. Wrap the head heavily so the reddish-brown thread stands out.

The second method of tying the Hendrickson Emerger is even easier than the first method. If you use this tying procedure you'll use the hackle for the tail, wing pad, and legs. Make certain that you tie in the hackle with its shiny side up and dull side down. The tip of the hackle becomes the tail of the emerger, the center of the hackle is the wing pad, and by teasing a few of the barbules from either side with a bodkin you have instant legs.

Try both methods of tying the Hendrickson Emerger.

Dressing: Hendrickson Emerger
Hook: Size 12 or 14 nymph hook.
Thread: Reddish-brown.
Tail: Barbules from a cree hackle (brown and lighter). For alternate method, tip of a furnace hackle (see step 4).
Body: Brownish-black angora or opossum (mix about eight parts of black with two parts of dark brown).
Wing pad: Dark part of furnace hackle.
Hackle: Brown hackle tips from the same hackle tips you used for the wing pad.

1. Tie in the thread behind the eye and wind back to the bend of the hook. Tie in about a half-dozen soft cree hackle barbules for the tail. Make a couple of wraps over the top of the butt section of the barbules to secure.
2. Dub some very dark brown opossum onto your tying thread and wrap the dubbing about halfway up the shank of the hook.
3. *Tie in about ten to twenty long furnace hackle barbules at the middle of the shank just in front of the completed back half of the body. You can substitute a dozen or so fibers from a dark gray mallard wing feather or a mottled brown secondary wing feather from a turkey. Tie them in by the butts. The tips of the wing feather will eventually form the legs of the emerger. Tie in at the butt section and with the tips of the barbules leaning back over the bend of the hook. Make a half-hitch with the bobbin. These barbules should be one-half to three-quarters of an inch long.*

4. *Alternate method: Take a large furnace hackle and tie it in by the tip at the bend of the hook. Have the dull side facedown and the tip of the hackle over the bend about half the length of the shank. That tip becomes the tail of the emerger. Dub the back half of the body. Make certain that you cover the hackle stem. Keep the hackle stem at the halfway point, add a five-inch piece of dark brown tying thread, and dub the front half of the body. Pull the hackle stem over top of the front half of the body and tie in at the eye. Rib the front half with the loose piece of tying thread, you left behind. After you've tied in the stem and clipped the excess, take a bodkin and tease a few of the hackle fibers from the hackle stem on the right and left.* **With one hackle you now have a tail, dark wing pad, and brown legs.**

5. Dub in the front half of the body with same dark brownish-black opossum, *but make it much more robust so the wing pad on top will suggest that the wing is about to split and the dun ready*

to appear. Wind up just in front of the eye.

6. *Pull the furnace hackle barbules up over the thorax (the front half of the body) and tie in just behind the eye. Don't cut off the tips.*

7. *Take about half of the tips of the barbules and divide them in two, making the legs on the right and left sides. After you've divided the barbules, wind in front of them to make the legs move back.*

8. *Note: If you use a short-nozzled bobbin (like the S&M bobbin), you can now use a whip-finish of sorts. It's really a series of half-hitches that do the same work as a whip-finish. If you don't use a short-nozzled bobbin, try the lower half of a ballpoint pen.* **Either of these two implements will work as a hackle guard and prevent you from crowding the hook eye.** *Make certain that you wind plenty of wraps of the reddish-brown tying thread on the head.*

9. Apply head cement.

THE PHEASANT-TAIL NYMPH

I have seven patterns that I resort to when there's no hatch on the water. These are my regular dependable patterns. I often quit if I catch no trout on these reliable patterns in an hour, confident that no fly will catch fish on that particular day. I constantly test new patterns to see if any of these will fit into my carefully chosen selection. One of those dependable seven is the beadhead Pheasant-Tail Nymph. This dark brown nymphal pattern copies plenty of naturals. If you look at a pale morning dun or sulphur nymph, you'll see that the Pheasant-Tail adequately copies both. It is especially effective in late spring and early summer when these two nymphs are most active.

The Pheasant-Tail performs well in the West. Our guide, Richie Montella, took my son, Bryan, and me through four or five riffles and pools on the Bighorn River until he told us to get out of the boat. Just in front of us, more than a dozen heavy browns fed on spent-winged pale morning spinners. Bryan and I caught fourteen trout on spentwing patterns that morning in an hour in that one productive stretch.

A few minutes later and a half-mile downriver, a hatch of pale morning duns appeared on the surface. Just in front of us more than a dozen heavy browns fed on emerging pale morning duns. Richie suggested a tandem rig made up of a Size 14 Pale Morning Dun dry fly and a Size 16 beadhead Pheasant-Tail Nymph. Bryan and I caught more than a dozen trout on that duo that morning in an hour. I'm certain that Pheasant-Tail produced that day because it copies the pale morning nymph.

The Pheasant-Tail produces trout in all areas of the United States and Canada. That same pattern caught plenty of trout even on Ontario's fantastic Grand River. Even though that river is heavily fished, the Pheasant-Tail caught trout—in fact, it was the only pattern that worked for me the entire weekend.

The Pheasant-Tail Nymph is extremely easy to tie. Use only three to five long pheasant tail fibers and tie these on Sizes 12 to 20 scud type hooks. I usually add about five to nine wraps of .005- or .010-inch lead wire to make the pattern sink more quickly.

If you've tied the Pheasant-Tail before, then you already know it has one inherent problem: After you catch a couple of trout, the pheasant-tail body tends to split. One way to overcome this is to use ribbing. Tie in a fine piece of gold wire and wind it in the opposite direction that you wrapped the pheasant-tail body. Follow the procedure in step 6, and you'll have an excellent Pheasant-Tail Nymph, minus the bead, that copies the sulphur and pale morning nymphs.

Dressing: Pheasant-Tail Nymph
Hook: Size 12 to 20 scud hook.
Bead: Copper.
Thread: Dark brown.
Tail: Pheasant tail fibers.
Body: Pheasant tail fibers ribbed with gold wire.
Hackle: Pheasant tail fibers.

1. *Place several appropriate-sized copper beads on a tube of wax. Move the beads on the wax until the smaller hole in each is facing upward. Place the point of the hook through the smaller hole while the bead is on the wax.*
2. Take four pheasant tail barbules and tie in the tips to make a tail. The tail should be not quite as long as the shank of the hook. Don't cut off the remaining pheasant tail fibers—you'll use them later.
3. Tie in a piece of fine gold wire at the tail.
4. *Twist the pheasant tail two or three times and wind up to the bead. Now rib the body with the gold wire in the opposite direction that you wound the pheasant tail.* **Twisting the pheasant tail and using the wire will help prevent the fragile pheasant-tail body from breaking. You can further protect the body by using head cement on it.**
5. *Tie in about a half-dozen pheasant tail fibers on the bottom just behind the bead. Tie more in on both the right and left sides. These fibers should*

be about half the length of the hook shank. **These form the legs of the nymph.**

6. *Optional: Dub enough of the soft pale gray feathers from the bottom of the pheasant tail (nearest the quill) to make two wraps just in front of the legs and behind the bead.* **Note: You can make an even more realistic Sulphur nymph by following the procedure here, but omitting the bead, adding the soft gray pheasant tail fibers, and wrapping a large head of yellow tying thread.**

7. Whip-finish and apply head cement.

THE QUIGLEY WIGGLER

Nine of us spent an enjoyable, memorable week at Anne Marie Lodge on the Minipi River system near Goose Bay, Labrador. A tremendous hatch of green drakes (*Hexagenia rigida*) appeared nightly and we caught trout on imitations of the dun and spinner. About the third day, the trout began feeding more on the nymph and emerger and less on the dun. The nine anglers went out on the lake and river in motorized canoes in the morning, came back to the lodge for dinner, and then went back out for the last two hours of daylight. In the evening we talked about the day's events and tied flies for tomorrow's fishing. All of the anglers noticed how violently the green drake nymph wiggled near the surface before it emerged into a dun. The discussion around the table that evening was how to copy the movement of the emerger with a fly. Everybody tossed out suggestions.

I sat down at the fly-tying vise, took three Size 16 wet-fly hooks, and began tying. On one hook I tied a brown tail with some brown opossum. On the second I dubbed some gray opossum and palmered a grizzly hackle. On the final hook I again tied in some brown opossum and a brown hackle. I then connected the three. Ed Quigley, one of the anglers at the lodge, suggested I call the final product the Quigley Wiggler.

To match any type of nymph, make a series of these in different colors. Connect two, three, or four sections together to match the nymph. You can make several tail sections, several gill sections, and several head sections. Make them in some of the more common nymph color combinations. You can then interchange these parts to match any emerging nymph—and you get lifelike movement to boot.

You are essentially tying one pattern on two, three, or four hooks. You get the added bonus that the pattern moves. Tie each section fully; that is, cover the shanks completely from the eye of the hook to the bend (even a bit beyond the bend on the front two hooks). By doing this you'll get a more completely dressed pattern.

If you bend the hooks to close the gap, do it carefully; I've had a couple of hooks break on me after I tied them. If you use a Size 16 Mustad 3906B hook, you'll have to force the point of one into the eye of another. Unless the laws require it, you need not close the gap.

Try the Quigley Wiggler when you encounter one of those large drake hatches—it will work for you.

Dressing: Quigley Wiggler (*Hexagenia rigida* or green drake)
Hooks: Size 14 to 18 wet-fly hooks.
Hook #1 (rear)
Thread: Brown 6/0.
Tail: Three brown hackle tips.
Body: Gray opossum.
Hackle: Grizzly.

Hook #2 (middle)
Thread: Gray 6/0.
Body: Gray opossum.
Hackle: Grizzly.
Hook #3 (front)
Thread: Brown 6/0.
Wing pad: Mallard quill sections.
Body: Reddish-brown opossum.
Hackle: Brown.

1. Take the barbs off three Size 16 hooks.
2. Take one hook and tie in three brown hackle tips to form the tail. Have them extend beyond the bend about one-half the length of the shank of the hook.
3. Tie in a grizzly hackle at the rear.
4. Dub in some gray opossum and wrap to the eye. (Dress all three hooks fully and completely from the bend of the hook to the eye.) Next, palmer the body about four or five times with the grizzly hackle. Tie off and clip the top of the hackle (optional).
5. *Take a second hook and tie the section that copies the gills of the nymph. Tie in a grizzly hackle at the bend of the hook. Dub the shank with gray opossum and palmer it with the grizzly hackle. Tie off and cut the hackle fibers off the top.*
6. *Take the third hook and add weight to the body. Wrap about ten turns of .010- or .005-inch wire on the hook.* **When you're retrieving this pattern and you vary the motion, the weight on the third hook will make the pattern move in a very lifelike fashion.** *Tie in a mallard quill section as a wing pad at the bend of the third hook. Have the shiny side of the mallard quill face upward and the tips of the quill facing toward the rear. Also tie in a brown hackle, which will become the legs. Dub reddish-brown opossum in front, then wrap the hackle three or four times up the body. Either cut the hackle off the top or pull some of the top hackle fibers to the right and left. Pull the wing case over the body and tie off.*

7. *Now connect the three pieces by putting the point of one hook through the eye of the next one. Crimp the gaps of the front two hooks.* **Be very careful if you crimp the gaps or you'll break the hook and undo everything you've done.** *Test a hook or two before you crimp a completed one. Make sure you take the barb off before you try this.*

THE MARCH BROWN NYMPH

Have you ever looked at a March brown nymph? Check the bottom or abdomen and you'll see a cream belly with distinct dark brown ribs. The natural larva is difficult to duplicate—unless you use the method for tying the March Brown Nymph below. But, does the pattern work? I've used it on many occasions—especially when a March brown hatch has appeared in mid to late May.

The March brown is often a sporadic emerger, sometimes appearing with a burst at dusk. The Delaware River holds a great March brown hatch. Without a hatch the Delaware River can be cantankerous and un-forgiving; with a hatch you can experience one of the best fishing trips of your life. I'll never forget that late May afternoon on the Delaware with Bob Sentiwany. I was completing the manuscript for my book *Pennsylvania Trout Streams and Their Hatches,* and I wanted to fish this river one more time to experience a hatch. Hatches on the river peak in late May. On that afternoon and evening, March browns appeared sporadically. The March Brown Nymph worked well that afternoon on those big rainbows.

Make certain that you pull the dark brown wool yarn tightly up and over the body. Tie it in one-half to two-thirds of the way up the shank of the hook. The wing pad should begin where you end the rear end of the body.

Dressing: March Brown Nymph
Hook: Size 12 or 14 nymph hook.
Thread: Dark brown.
Tail: Dark brown hackle or dark mottled brown turkey.

Body: Cream opossum for the belly and dark brown wool or angora yarn for the back.

Wing pad: Mottled brown turkey quill section.

Hackle: Dark brown hackle.

1. *Optional: Tie in a piece of .010-inch lead wire on the right and left sides of the hook shank. Wrap the tying thread over the wire tightly and thoroughly to keep it in place. Add some superglue.*

2. *Wind the tying thread to the bend of the hook and tie in a few dark brown hackle or mottled brown turkey wing barbules for the tail. Make the tail a bit shorter than the shank of the hook. Tie in a piece or two (depending on the size of the material and the hook) of dark brown yarn just in front of the tail. Make sure you tie the*

brown yarn on top. Also tie in a six-inch piece of dark brown tying thread and leave it at the tail. Use the create-a-loop method: Make a loop at the bend of the hook with your tying thread. After you've made a three-inch loop, tie it off at the bend by winding over it with the regular tying thread still attached to the bobbin. After the loop is secured, cut one end close to the body. **Now you have a six-inch piece of tying thread, secured and ready to use to rib the body.**

3. Dub some cream opossum or angora and wind one-half to two-thirds of the way up the shank. *Now pull the dark brown wool or angora yarn over the top. Tie in with the regular tying thread. Rib the body four times with the six-inch piece of tying thread you left at the hook bend.* **This will secure the back and give the ribbing effect to the abdomen and back.**

4. *At this point tie in two dark brown turkey quill sections for the wing pad and a dark brown hackle for the legs. Tie the quill section so the tip of the feather points backward and the dull side is facing down.* ***The wing pad will be much wider and more lifelike if you tie in two sections.***

5. Dub the remaining front of the body liberally with cream fur.

6. Wind the hackle forward to the eye and tie in. Clip the hackle on the top or pull the top right hackle to the right and to the left and bring the turkey quill up and over the front third of the body.

7. Tie in and whip-finish.

THE SWIMMING EPHEMERA NYMPH

I've indicated many times that I've had several innovative fly tiers help me with this book. One of those contributors is Kurt Thomas of Ridgway, Pennsylvania. He's shown me two of his innovative patterns and did a spectacular job with his illustrations in this book. Kurt has tied flies for more than thirty years—he tied flies before he fly fished. He guides clients through GDP Guide Service on central Pennsylvania waters.

If you remember in *How to Catch More Trout,* I said I often rate the fly fishers I know with ten being the highest. Kurt is a ten.

Kurt is innovative when tying flies. He's always experimenting with new patterns and materials. He came up with the Swimming Ephemera Nymph about five years ago. It's not difficult to tie, but it is highly effective, especially when a green, brown, or yellow drake emerges. It is lifelike and Kurt says that trout lose their timidity when they see this pattern.

What's innovative about this fly? It looks "buggy" and has a perfect silhouette. Who ever heard of taking a bunch of pale gray or tan marabou, wetting it, and making a knot in the material? That's the beauty of this pattern.

Marabou, however, is somewhat fragile. To help overcome this, Kurt adds a drop of cement to the knot.

Although we're tying a pattern to copy the green drake nymph, you can use this same pattern—with a few changes in color—to copy any of the burrowing nymphs.

Dressing: Swimming Ephemera Nymph
Hook: Mustad 3906B, Size 12.
Thread: Light tan, 8/0.
Body (and tail): Light creamish-gray marabou; light creamish-gray rabbit, dubbed.
Gills: Aftershaft feather.
Wing case: Pheasant tail fibers.
Legs: Mottled brown hen-pheasant fibers.

1. Add about five turns of .005-inch-thick lead or X-ray foil at the front of the hook.
2. Flatten the lead with a pliers. Overlap with tying thread and add a drop of superglue.
3. Wind the tying thread back to the bend of the hook. Take about ten barbules of marabou, wet them and make a knot in them about one-quarter inch from the tips. You can also use a leg tool to make the knot. Add a drop of cement to the knotted area.

4. *Take the ten barbules of knotted marabou and extend them about two times the length of the shank of the hook. Tie in just in front of the bend of the hook. The knotted end should extend out over the hook.*

5. Dub in light tannish-gray rabbit and make two turns directly in front of the tied-in marabou. *Push the remainder of the dubbed rabbit down the thread—you'll use this later.*

6. Take a secondary shaft or after-shaft feather of a pheasant sad-dle (that's the little fuzzy gray feather behind the stronger-col-ored one). Lay the feather with the tips extending backward and almost to the tail. Clip off the excess aftershaft butt section and tie off. *Don't throw the re-maining aftershaft away—you'll use it later.*

7. Make two more wraps with the dubbed rabbit in front of the tied-off aftershaft. *Slide down the excess dubbing to use later.*

8. Take the remainder of the aftershaft feather and cut a V-shaped notch out of the remaining tip. Tie in near the butt of the aftershaft and with the tips extending toward the tail. **This is the gill section of the nymph.**

9. Make two more wraps with the rabbit dubbing.

10. Take ten strands of pheasant tail and tie in on both sides. **This will become the wing case.**

11. *Loosely dub more rabbit fur so this section is fairly large.* **This enlarged section will suggest an emerging nymph.**

12. *Pull the pheasant tail fibers over top of the enlarged section and tie in.*

13. Take a dozen mottled brown hen-pheasant or partridge barbules. Make them as long as the shank of the hook. Tie in on either side of the hook. Make a couple of wraps and slide underneath. **These become the legs.**

14. Tie off and cement.

I hope you learn some new tricks when you tie these patterns. All of these patterns are quite productive and relatively easy to tie.

3

Wet Flies

9. How to make lifelike eyes out of monofilament line (Bugskin Crayfish, step 4)
10. How to tell exactly how many wraps and what weight lead you have on a pattern (Green Weenie, steps 1 and 4)
11. How to make a twisted tail on a streamer (Green Weenie, step 2)

We have already seen what emerger, nymph, dry fly, and spentwing patterns are designed to copy. What the heck does a wet fly imitate? The wet fly copies a host of insects and phases of the life cycle. First, it adequately copies the mayflies and caddisflies that emerge on the bottom of a stream, river, or lake and swim to the top. Hatches such as the quill Gordon, pink lady, and many others change from duns to spinners near the bottom and swim to the top as duns. The wet fly was the earliest type of emerger pattern. The wet fly also copies crippled duns that have sunk beneath the surface. Wet flies also copy other important aquatic food like cress bugs, crayfish, and freshwater shrimp.

FISHING THE WET FLY

For the first two decades of my fly-fishing career, I almost totally relied on wet flies to catch trout. Why not? They consistently caught trout for me. But in the late 1960s, after reading Schwiebert's *Matching the Hatch,* I became one of those match-the-hatch freaks who would wait for hours until a trout rose. On some summer evenings I wouldn't fish for hours; I just sat there and waited—and waited. In the early 1990s, I saw the light and once again began relying on wet flies. Let me explain.

An incident on Montana's Bighorn River changed my way of fishing forever. I mentioned it first in *Patterns, Hatches, Tactics and Trout.* Our guide for that trip, Richie Montella, saw that I had difficulty fishing a wet fly, so he rigged up my line so I had a dry fly closest to my reel and two and a half feet beyond that he placed a weighted wet fly. I began casting this tandem arrangement and immediately had trouble. Casting two patterns—especially with one being weighted—presented some interest-ing problems. After about a half-hour of clumsily casting the duo, I got onto the process and felt comfortable with the setup. More important, I began catching trout on the wet fly. Since that introduction to using the tandem, I have used the same setup almost continuously. Consequently, the wet flies I tie are often those that work well on a tandem setup. If you haven't used this technique, you should.

If you're dead set against using two patterns and you want to use a wet fly effectively, then try using one with a poly yarn strike indica-tor. I feel certain a poly strike indicator is the next best thing to using the tandem.

What patterns work best as part of a tandem? Some of the more bizarre patterns—those that don't necessarily imitate any particular in-sect—seem to work well. I have one I call I'm Not Sure. We'll look at this pattern and others.

Does a wet fly sometimes work during a hatch? Two of the largest trout I ever caught during a hatch were taken on a dry fly that I pur-posely sank during the hatch. Both trout took a dry-fly Green Drake pat-tern in the height of the hatch, but just under the surface.

TYING THE WET FLY

Diametrically opposed to the dry fly, you want the wet fly to sink—often as quickly as possible. I believe the quicker the pattern sinks the more effective it is. Use heavy hooks like Mustad's 3906 or 3906B, hen feath-ers with more webbing, and body materials like wool, angora, and muskrat. I hate adding split shot to the leader to get wet flies deeper and feel there's a better way. If you want to hasten the sinking process, add a few turns of weight to the body of the wet fly when you tie it.

What has changed wet-fly fishing more than any one other item in the past decade? It's got to be the bead. Beads also help to get patterns to the bottom, especially tungsten beads. They're extremely heavy and take a wet fly to the bottom quickly. You'll see later in this chapter how important it is to get the pattern deep when you fish for steelhead. Don't use tungsten beads if you plan to use a dry fly in a tandem setup.

Beads, however, can cause tying problems. First, you'll probably lose plenty of them on the floor of your tying area. Use a tube of wax and place several beads on it. Second, have you noticed that after a few uses the bead become dull? You can prevent this discoloration by covering the bead with epoxy. Epoxy will prevent the bead from moving back and also protects the shine.

Beads also help hide the lead wire wrapped on the shank. I use lead wire on my Glo Bug to get it deeper, faster. Follow the directions for placing wire on the Glo Bug, and push the wire up and under the bead.

In this chapter you'll learn several new techniques for tying wet flies. Have you had the bead slip back on the shank of a wet fly? You'll learn how to prevent this when you tie the terrific new pattern called the Zebra Midge. Have you ever wondered whether a pattern you're using has weight added to the shank, and if it does just how many wraps of what weight lead were used? You'll learn how to keep a record of the weight you use when you tie I'm Not Sure and the Green Weenie. Why is this important? Where you fish the pattern (depth) is one of four key ingredients I mention in *How to Catch More Trout*. If you know the number of wraps and the size of the weight you are using, you can more easily control the depth.

I'M NOT SURE

The thing looks like a Green Weenie but it has a bright red fluorescent body. What do I call it? It should probably be called a Red Weenie or Red Worm. What does the pattern imitate? I'm not sure. Fly fishers on the San Juan River in New Mexico have used a version, called the San Juan Red Worm, for years with unbelievable success.

Fred Bridge of York, Pennsylvania, told me about the pattern. I first tried the fly on a lake near Phoenix, Arizona. It was a slow day. Ten other anglers lined the Butcher Jones Cove area on Saguaro Lake. No one caught anything for more than an hour. Then I decided to test the new pattern. On the fifth cast a trout struck but I missed it. A few more casts and another missed trout. Finally, I hooked a fish—then another and still another.

One of the anglers on the far shore blurted out, "What are you using?"

"I'm Not Sure," I yelled to him.

The angler yelled back in an even more determined tone, "What pattern are you using?"

I yelled again, "I'm Not Sure."

Finally, he had enough and waded over to me to look at the pattern. I showed him the bright red fly and told him I call it I'm Not Sure. He looked at the pattern, shook his head, and waded back to his fishing location.

In the few years that I've used this pattern, it has seemed to catch a higher number of rainbow than brown trout. Remember that when you use I'm Not Sure.

Christopher Fisher (left) is ready to release a trout caught on a large red fly, I'm Not Sure, while Bryan Meck (right) looks on.

I'm Not Sure works well in streams and rivers with high runoff. I'll never forget talking to Andy Sheffler after a day of fishing. The preceding two days had deposited more than two inches of rain on central Pennsylvania streams. Andy said that nothing—I mean nothing—worked for him in the high water. "I tried every colored pattern—except red," Andy said after an exhausting day of fishing high water. Guess what? I'm Not Sure caught trout in that high water. Andy also used one of these red patterns the next day and caught trout.

I think the tail is important on the I'm Not Sure and the Green Weenie. The tail tends to make the pattern wiggle as it drifts with the current.

Dressing: I'm Not Sure
Hook: Mustad 9672, Size 10 to 12.
Thread: Fiery red.
Body: Fluorescent red chenille (medium or small).

1. *Add weight to the body. Make ten, fifteen, or twenty wraps with the lead wire. Use a different color tying thread for each pattern you tie that has a different number of wraps of lead. Keep a sheet of paper in the box where you place these and you'll always know how much weight each pattern has. For example, with this pattern you might use red tying thread for ten wraps, pink thread for fifteen, and orange for twenty.*
2. Tie in medium or small fluorescent red chenille.
3. *Make a loop in the tail. Do this by doubling the chenille.* **This loop in the tail acts as a rudder and moves the pattern from side to side.** *It should be about one-third the length of the shank of the hook.*
4. Now wind the remainder of the chenille up to the eye, tie off, and cement.

THE GREEN WEENIE

I'll always recall the first time I saw an angler cast a Green Weenie. That introduction to this effective pattern occurred on the Loyalhanna Creek in Ligonier in southwestern Pennsylvania. It was my first day out, and I was working on the manuscript for *Pennsylvania Trout Streams and Their Hatches.* The late Russ Mowry, a famous fly tier and a terrific person, fished with Tim Shaffer and Ken Igo. I sat on the bank of the stream that March afternoon and watched the trio catch twenty-five trout while six other anglers around them caught nothing. Since that day back in 1988, I have made certain I always carry a good supply of Green Weenies.

Mary Kuss of Media, Pennsylvania, recalls an instance where the Green Weenie worked well for her several years ago. On ten casts Mary caught a half-dozen trout. Finally one of the anglers nearby came up to Mary and asked her what she was using. Mary showed the angler the Green Weenie and he walked away mumbling to himself. Barry Staats, owner of the Sporting Gentleman in Media, Pennsylvania, tells me he sells thousands of these patterns annually in his fly shop.

The Green Weenie seems to work better on some trout streams than others. I use the pattern all winter on the Salt River near Phoenix, Arizona. Fred Brauburger, of nearby Scottsdale, and I caught 135 trout one day on the Salt River. The majority of those trout hit the Green Weenie.

Several years back I opened the New York trout season on Irondequoit Creek near Rochester, New York. We didn't arrive until some of the anglers had already left. I tied on a Green Weenie and fished in a pool with five other anglers. While those five bait fishers watched, I caught a half-dozen trout. Several anglers came over to me to ask what I was using.

The Green Weenie works well on far-western rivers. I first used the pattern on a McKenzie River float trip with an expert guide, Ken Helfrich of Springfield, Oregon. The river ran at least a foot above its normal flow for early May, and no pattern I used seemed to catch trout. Then, in a fit of frustration, I tied on a Green Weenie. In the next three hours I caught more than twenty trout and the day was transformed into one of those memorable trips. Was Ken impressed with the pattern? He asked me to give him a few for his customers he planned to guide the next day.

The Green Weenie is so simple to tie—but it works. You'll use a twisted tail and a color key for the head. With this color key you can tell not only the number of wraps but also the weight of the pattern.

Dressing: Green Weenie
Hook: Mustad 9672, Size 10.
Tail: A loop of small or medium chartreuse chenille.
Body: Chartreuse chenille, small or medium.

1. *Use black, chartreuse, yellow, olive, or tan tying thread. Use black for .005-inch, chartreuse for .010-inch, yellow for .015-inch, and tan for .020-inch lead. Whichever color tying thread you use, make fifteen wraps with it. This way you'll know exactly how many wraps and what weight lead you have on each pattern. Or, you can use the same diameter lead and use black thread for ten wraps, red for fifteen, and green for twenty. Or, you can tie a bicolor head and know how many wraps and what weight lead you're using.*
2. *Spin a six-inch piece of chenille by hand. Move the two ends together and place the twisted part as the tail. Make the tail about one-quarter the length of the hook shank.* **That loop becomes the short tail for the Green Weenie and helps move the pattern from side to side.**
3. Wrap the chenille up to the eye of the hook.
4. **Place a sheet of paper in the fly box where you store these ties so you know what color thread is used for what weight.**

THE GLO BUG

There's no way in the world that I'd ever use anything like Sucker Spawn or a Glo Bug. For years I hated even the thought of using one of these patterns. Let's call a spade a spade: Glo Bugs are the fly fisher's answer to the bait fisher's salmon egg, and I refused to try one. Then one day I fished with an outstanding fly fisher and guide, Bruce Matolyak, on a private section of a limestone stream. While I caught no trout in a one-hour period, Bruce caught a half-dozen—all over eighteen inches long. When he showed me the Glo Bug he was using, I finally gave in and tried one. In the next two hours I released a half-dozen trout—including a hefty brown over twenty inches long—and all were caught on a Glo Bug pattern. That changed my thinking on the Glo Bug. There are times that the Glo Bug—and only the Glo Bug—works to perfection.

One winter day on the Red River in New Mexico proved the merits of the beadhead Glo Bug. Four of us headed down the steep gorge to the river below at about 10 A.M. It took us two hours to reach our final destination at the bottom of the gorge. I began casting a Glo Bug and immediately caught several trout. The final trout, a twenty-inch cuttbow, swam from one small pool to another after it took the Glo Bug. Before we retraced our steps back up the steep gorge and to the car, all four of us anglers had caught trout on the beadhead Glo Bug. It really does work all across the United States.

But there's an inherent problem with the Glo Bug: Sometimes it takes forever to sink the pattern. I've used the same fly for a half hour and it still floated after all of that time. I most often fish the pattern behind a floating dry fly on a tandem rig, so I don't want to add a lead shot to the leader. What do I do? I always add a bead and weight to the pattern. That bead might suggest a yolk in the egg, but whatever it looks like it really works. The bead helps sink the pattern quickly. However, even with the addition of the bead, the pattern sometimes refuses to sink very quickly. How do I overcome this tendency? I now add six to nine turns of .005-inch lead wire to the shank before I add the Glo Bug material. I shove the wire up under the bead, and then make several turns with the fly-tying thread and add a drop of superglue to keep it in place. The Glo Bug now sinks rapidly, but the dry fly or other strike indicator still floats in full view.

I use bright red tying thread and prefer cream Glo Bug material. There are many ways to tie a Glo Bug. I prefer to place two pieces of cream Glo Bug yarn on the hook shank, one on either side, and tie both on at the same time.

Dressing: Glo Bug

Hook: Size 12 or 14 scud hook.
Bead: Copper.
Thread: Fluorescent orange-red.
Body: Glo Bug material (I prefer cream). Add a small piece of bright orange to imitate the egg sac.

1. *Follow the procedure for the Pheasant-Tail Nymph in Chapter 3 for placing a bead on the hook.*
2. *Wrap six to nine turns of .005-inch lead wire and shove it up and under the bead. Now wrap the red tying thread just behind the Glo Bug to prevent the lead from moving back. Also add a drop or two of superglue to the bead.*
3. Wind the fluorescent red tying thread about one-third of the way back on the hook shank. Tie in two three-quarter-inch-long pieces of Glo Bug material, one on either side of the hook. Make a couple of tight turns with the thread and tie off.
4. Pull the material on top and cut closely. Shape roughly, but carry a scissors with you on the stream and clip after you've fished the pattern for a few minutes. ***After the material is wet it's much easier to shape into a ball.***

THE ZEBRA MIDGE

Some of the simplest fly patterns to tie are also the most productive. I'm convinced that many of the more complicated, tedious ties catch fishermen but not fish. Some of the least complicated flies catch fish. Let me explain.

I first found out about a great new pattern when I fished the Lee's Ferry section of the Colorado River in northern Arizona. Frank Nofer, an attorney from Philadelphia, Pennsylvania, and I arrived at the boat launching site at 7 A.M. to meet our guide, Chad Bayles. We traveled up-river several miles before Chad guided the boat to shore and asked us to try a productive-looking riffle.

For the first half-hour I didn't catch a thing on the Size 14 beadhead Pheasant-Tail Nymph, but things were about to change—and change quickly. I tied on a Size 18 Zebra Midge two feet behind a Size 12 Patriot dry fly. The dry fly kept the Zebra Midge from going too deep and it also acted as a strike indicator. On the second cast, a fourteen-inch rainbow quickly sucked in the midge imitation—not bad for the new pattern. Three more casts and I hooked a twenty-inch rainbow. Chad and Frank had the same success with the pattern, and for the next two hours one of the three of us had a trout on almost continuously.

Jerry Meck lands a heavy rainbow on a Zebra Midge on the Colorado River at Lee's Ferry in Arizona.

Why did that simple pattern work so well on this river? The Colorado at Lee's Ferry has more than thirty different chironomid species. Almost every day of the year you'll see heavy midge hatches appearing just about all day long. The Zebra Midge covers many of these emerging midges.

But would this same pattern be effective across the United States, specifically in the East and Mid-west? I'd soon find out. I was anxious to test this pattern back East.

For the past twenty years I have opened the Pennsylvania trout season on Bald Eagle Creek in central Pennsylvania. What can I say—it's a tradition. The stream has some good early-season hatches but also plenty of angling pressure. When we arrived we noted that the stream was as low as it ever was on opening day. For the first hour I drifted a heavy Woolly Bugger without getting even one strike. Then I moved to a pool

Lee's Ferry on the Colorado River holds more than thirty different midge species.

where they must have planted trout. Ten bait fishermen lined both shores and gave me little room to cast. I moved to the lower end of the pool, and stood and watched for a few minutes. I noticed a trout feeding occasionally at the tail of the pool; then I saw several other trout feeding just a few feet upstream from where I stood. I saw only midges on the surface and decided to give the Zebra Midge a try. I tied it on a tandem two feet behind a Size 12 Patriot dry fly. After only a couple of drifts the Patriot sank and I set the hook on a twelve-inch brown trout. During the next hour I landed nine more trout on that Size 18 pattern while the bait fishermen landed only a couple. Soon they were saying nasty remarks like "Why don't you fish some other stretch?"

Don't overlook the Zebra Midge during the fall and winter months. Many of the country's top streams hold great midge hatches every day throughout the fall and winter. The Zebra Midge should work well then.

The Zebra Midge is so productive and easy to tie that even if you've never tied a fly before you'll be able to tie this one. All you need is a hook, a bead, black tying thread, and fine silver wire. It's so easy that I've had anglers who had never tied before finish one of the patterns in a couple of minutes.

Remember the Zebra Midge when you are confronted with the problem of pattern selection or you're fishing one of those heavily fished streams. It is an extremely productive pattern for the West and it works equally well in the East and Midwest. It will definitely work for you.

The Zebra Midge is a simple pattern that sinks quickly. Its simple form and body shape help the pattern sink quickly. Make certain that you use a very fine wire to rib the body.

Dressing: Zebra Midge

Hook: Size 16 to 20 shrimp/caddis hook.
Bead: Brass (for black body) or copper (for chocolate and olive body).
Thread: Black, chocolate brown, or olive 6/0, not pre-waxed.
Body: Black, chocolate brown, or olive tying thread.
Ribbing: Fine silver wire (for black body) or fine copper wire (for chocolate brown and olive body).

1. *Place several three-thirty-seconds-inch brass beads on a tube of wax. The wax holds the beads in place. Move the beads so the smaller opening is on top.*
2. Make certain you put the point of the hook through the smaller opening on the bead.
3. Tie in the black thread behind the eye and wind back just beyond the bend of the hook.
4. Tie in a two-inch-long piece of fine silver wire at the bend. Now wind the black tying thread toward the eye. Make certain that you cover the shank of the hook completely with tying thread.
5. Rib the body with the fine silver wire. Rib the body fairly closely so that you make about seven wraps with the wire. **By creating a smooth body with little friction this pattern sinks quickly.**
6. *Don't cut off the silver wire too closely. Leave a short piece of wire to help prevent the bead from moving back over the hook.*
7. Tie off the wire just behind the bead and *add a drop of superglue at the bead to hold it in place.* Or you can cover the entire bead with five-minute epoxy. The latter (see the Golden Shiner in Chapter 9) will build a protective covering for the bead and hold it in place.

8. Whip-finish.

THE MARCH BROWN

Earlier I said that I seldom use wet flies. That's not totally accurate, especially taking into account the first few years I fly fished. How did I start fly fishing? I tried casting an old telescoping metal "fly rod" and used snelled wet flies. I caught plenty of trout on a March Brown wet fly during those formative years. Snelled flies came with a leader already attached to the fly and a loop on the other end of the leader so you could attach it to your tippet. If you're old enough to remember these patterns, you'll also recall that they were extremely effective. One of my favorite wet flies was called a March Brown. Many of the old-fashioned wet flies are now almost extinct; with the advent of emergers, wet flies are almost a thing of the past. Wet flies, however, still produce trout, and they too can be called emerger patterns. The March Brown was very productive fifty years ago, and it still is today.

If you want a really full wing for the March Brown and other large wet flies, you can follow the procedure for the Salmon Fly (Chapter 6) and the Elk Hop (Chapter 4). In those latter two you'll see how one wing is placed in front of another.

Dressing: March Brown
Hook: Size 12 to 14 wet-fly hook.
Thread: Dark brown olive 6/0.
Body: Tan opossum, ribbed with dark brown tying thread.
Wings: Mallard flank feather dyed dark brown.
Hackle: Dark brown hen hackle.

1. Tie in three or four barbules of brown hen hackle for the tail. Tie in a dark brown piece of thread just in front of the tail or use the create-a-loop method.
2. Dub in tan opossum and wind it three-quarters of the way up the hook.
3. *Tie in about ten to fifteen barbules on the left side of the fly just behind the hook eye. This hackle should be about three-quarters of the length of the shank of the hook. Make several turns with the tying thread, then gently ro-*

tate those hackle fibers down and under the hook. **This method, first showed to me by George Harvey, moves the hackle underneath quickly and easily.**

4. Tie in ten to fifteen fibers from a dark mallard flank feather on top of the body just in front of the hackle. Make several wraps of tying thread to hold the wing on top.
5. Whip-finish and cement.

THE BUGSKIN CRAYFISH

I've seen everything in the way of materials used to tie flies. I once had a fly tier give me a fly that had a body made from discarded cassette tape—you know, that tape that you see strewn along our highways. Talk about recycling—that's one of the best. But wait a minute: Have you ever heard of effective patterns tied from tanned leather? Enter Chuck Furimsky and his leather shop. Chuck has tied flies for forty

Chuck Furimsky ties his famous Bugskin Crayfish.

years; thirty-five of those years he has also owned and operated a leather shop.

Chuck also operates, along with Barry Serviente, Fly Fishing Shows throughout the United States. He offers programs in Seattle; San Raphael, California; Denver; Somerset, New Jersey; Boston; Charlotte, North Carolina; and College Park, Maryland. Chuck's son, Ben, ties with Bugskin at the Somerset Show. If you see a man wandering around these shows with a handlebar moustache and a flag tie, that's Chuck.

In those thirty-five years, Chuck has found that leather is extremely pliable, strong, flexible, and tough. About a decade ago, he found a special machine that could thin the leather for better tying, and he began making patterns that had leather as the main component. He ties beetles, nymphs, baitfish, and crayfish with leather. He found that these patterns were not only productive but durable. He's caught one hundred trout on some of the patterns and they're still intact. He prefers using tanned lambskin, sheepskin, and deerskin. He calls his product Bugskin, and it's available in selected fly shops and catalogs.

One of his all-time favorite patterns is the Bugskin Crayfish. It is a truly lifelike and highly productive pattern. If you want to get this pattern to sink quickly, add some weight to the body. It is possibly the most complicated of all the ties included in this book, but once you tie one of these patterns you'll want to make more.

Dressing: Bugskin Crayfish
Hook: Use a hook like the Mustad 79580, Size 6, 8 or 10.
Thread: Black 6/0.
Carapace (back) and claws: Mottled brown Bugskin.
Body: Tan, olive, or light brown dubbing like opossum or angora.
Ribbing: Medium copper wire.
Head: Red squirrel.
Hackle: Brown hackle.

1. Remember: The front of the crayfish is tied on the rear of the hook. Note: You can add weight to the body of this pattern by winding .010-inch lead around the shank. Cut out the carapace (make certain that you've shaped a point on the front end of the crayfish so it is easier to tie in) and the claws to fit the size of the hook. Glue the Bugskin together with contact cement so the suede sides are hidden. This will produce a pattern with the claws the same on both sides.

2. Tie on the black thread and wind back to the bend of the hook. Take about ten strands of red squirrel tail and tie in at the bend. The material should extend beyond the bend about half the length of the hook shank.

3. Tie in the Bugskin carapace by the point at the bend of the hook. Remember, the side that is down will eventually be the top side.

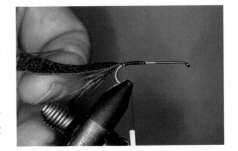

4. *Melt both ends of a one-inch piece of 20- to 25-pound-test monofilament to form two eyes.*

Flatten the sides of the mono with pliers so they stay put when you tie them in. Don't apply the eyes yet. Darken the eyes with a black permanent marker.

5. Begin dubbing the head of the crayfish at the rear of the hook. Dub one-third of the way up the hook.

6. Place the eyes so the two beads face back and extend just one-eighth of an inch beyond the bend. Wind some dubbing over and around the eyes to position them and hold them more securely in place.

7. Continue to form the head with dubbing by winding to a point where you'll tie in the pincers. Tie a pincer arm on each side. These pincer arms should be tapered so they are easy to tie in. The pincers should extend backward and beyond the hook bend one-quarter of an inch.

8. Dub over and around the pincers in a figure-eight to hold them in position.

9. Dub the remainder of the shank, and then work the thread back to the midsection. Now tie in the copper wire.

10. Tie in a brown hackle (shiny side forward) at the same location you've tied in the wire.

11. Cover the wraps of thread with a light dubbing and move the thread forward slightly toward the eye of the hook.

12. Make three or four turns with the hackle from the pincers to the tying thread and tie off. Weave wire through the hackle and tie off with tying thread. Don't wrap the wire to the eye of the hook. You'll use the wire to rib the Bugskin back later.

13. Slightly dub the tail area (front of the hook) and end up at the eye.

14. Apply a layer of contact cement to the top side of the Bugskin carapace and the top of the dubbed body.

15. Carefully position the Bugskin body over top of the dubbed body and press into place. The contact cement will hold the carapace in place.

16. Rib the back of the Bugskin with the copper wire. Tie off the wire at the eye.

17. *Pull the tail of the Bugskin and find the eye of the hook. Carefully poke a hole in the tail with a bodkin through the eye.* Enlarge this hole carefully with one scissor blade and place the hole through the eye of the hook. Trim the Bugskin tail.

Note: In *How to Catch More Trout,* I list "where you fish the pattern" or depth as one of the most important criteria to help you succeed in trout fishing. One easy way to get a pattern deep as quickly as possible is to use tungsten beads. Following is an account of how effective these can be, especially when fishing for steelhead.

TUNGSTEN GLO BUG, TUNGSTEN BLACK AND GREEN CADDIS FOR GREAT LAKES STEELHEAD

By Bryan Meck

March 3, 2002, started off rather calmly for Tom Hutchison of Macedon, New York. We set off on our drive to Sandy Creek in search of Lake Ontario steelhead, which were coming into the creeks on their annual spawning run. Sandy Creek is located on the west side of Rochester off the Lake Ontario Parkway, in Hamlin. We had planned to fish another one of the Lake Ontario tributaries that day, but lake-effect squalls had made us change our plans the evening before. We arrived at Sandy to see large chunks of ice flowing downstream. The air temperature was 27 degrees Fahrenheit and the water temperature was 35. It was sunny, but other than that it was probably a better day for tying flies than fishing them. As we stared down the stream, a typical western New York lake-enhanced squall drove the sun away. Should we head home? We decided to fish for a while with one eye on the sky. Tom asked what I was going to use and I commented that if there were any cold-blooded steelhead in the creek they would be right on the bottom, using as little energy as possible.

I quickly tied on a tungsten bead–head Black Caddis. I separate my steelhead patterns by size of the bead: regular (³⁄₃₂-, ⅛-, ³⁄₁₆-, and ⁵⁄₃₂-inch) and then tungsten (³⁄₃₂-, ⅛-, ³⁄₁₆-, and ⁵⁄₃₂-inch) over traditional hook sizes. I have found that using the correct weight is more important to success than using a Size 12 or 14 pattern. The reason why is there usually is not a hatch to match. You have to match the depth more than the hatch in order to catch steelhead. This doesn't mean you can use a Size 2 nymph in low, clear water, however.

Tom and I quickly hooked and released two small fish. Tom then landed a large, ten-pound male, and I coaxed an eight-pound female to take the Tungsten Black Caddis. I hate to use split shot: I can't roll cast as well, the line loses some of its strength, and the shot can slide down the line to the fly. Tungsten beads enable me to weight the fly and to keep it in the steelhead's strike zone longer. I often switch to the same fly pattern, only using a heavier or lighter bead depending on the pool that I am fishing or on water conditions. Be ready to change your pattern and carry a wide variety of weighted nymphs, mostly black, green, and brown, in Sizes 6 to 14. Great Lakes steelhead fishing can be some of the most rod-bending excitement you can have. It can also be some of the most frustrating. Don't be afraid to change patterns regularly to make sure you are fishing the right depth.

Use the same tying materials and procedures for making the regular Glo Bug and Black Caddis patterns, only use tungsten beads.

Dressing: Tungsten Black Caddis
Hook: Size 6 to 14 scud hook.
Bead: Tungsten.
Body: Black angora or opossum.

1. *Use a tungsten bead to fit the size of the hook (see the text).* **Don't add any additional weight—this bead should take the pattern to the bottom.**
2. Dub black opossum and wind to the hook eye.
3. Make one turn of peacock herl just behind the bead.
4. Whip-finish.

    That's it—it's that easy. By now you've accumulated a few more techniques such as those used to tie the Bugskin Crayfish and the Glo Bug. Try fishing the patterns you've tied. The Zebra Midge has consistently been one of the top flies I use.

4

Terrestrials

What are terrestrials? Why are they an important part of the arsenal of the fly fisher? Terrestrials are land-born insects that find their way onto the surface of streams, rivers, and lakes. Some of these terrestrials, such as the flying ant, cicada, and others, can create heavy feeding frenzies by their sheer numbers. Other terrestrials that often find their way onto the surface include grasshoppers, crickets, ants, and beetles. All of these become especially important in June, July, and August.

FISHING TERRESTRIALS

It's July or August and many of your favorite hatches have ended for the year. What do you do now? What patterns work on these hot summer days when no hatch appears? If you're fly fishing any stream or river that meanders through a meadow, a grasshopper imitation might prove effective. Even though it occurred more than twenty years ago I still remember that trip to the Arkansas River in the Brown Canyon area in Colorado. A grasshopper pattern saved the day for me—a day when no other pattern seemed to work. No insect appeared on the surface and no trout rose on that hot July afternoon, but the minute I began casting a hopper pattern trout chased it. The more I dragged that hopper across the surface the more violent the strikes were.

Just ask guides like Craig Shuman and Jack Mitchell on central Washington's Yakima River what they use in late summer. They'll tell you how effective grasshopper patterns are. Every day for several weeks, Craig and Jack find that hopper patterns work extremely well along the banks of the Yakima.

Then there's an unusual occurrence on or around August 25 on many Eastern trout waters. Almost like clockwork you'll find winged ants falling on the surface of many trout streams. They fall in such great numbers that they create a feeding frenzy that can last for hours. If you carry dark brown and black ant patterns in Sizes 18, 20, and 22, you'll find unbelievable matching-the-terrestrial episodes in late August.

You'll also find many other terrestrial patterns effective in July and August. Beetle and caterpillar imitations also work well at this time. I've even used white moth patterns to copy the adult of the spanworm caterpillar.

Terrestrials are often the patterns of choice when I fish small streams in midsummer. George Harvey often slaps his ant or beetle pattern onto the surface of these small streams. Unlike mayflies, stoneflies, and caddisflies, terrestrials often fall onto the surface from a distance and their sudden relocation often makes a more showy appearance than do aquatic insects emerging from the bottom of the stream. Try slapping the pattern if you find no takers when your terrestrial lands perfectly. Fish the banks and brush along the stream or river thoroughly. Since winds often transport terrestrials, fish these flies frequently when you encounter a breezy day.

Tandem Connection

In *How to Catch More Trout,* I mentioned that the depth you fish a pattern is one of the most important ingredients in fly fishing. Will trout take a pattern on the surface, subsurface, or on the bottom? The question of depth also goes for land-born insects. Not all terrestrials are taken on the surface; many beetles are found in the water continuously, and ants sink underneath after floating through a pool or two.

There's also a problem with fishing a dark colored terrestrial pattern; it is extremely difficult to follow on the surface. Enter the tandem setup. How can you possibly use a tandem connection with terrestrials? Ants and beetles ride low in the water. Even if you add a drop of orange or red paint, a bright feather on top as George Harvey does, or a short fluorescent post, you'll often have difficulty following the pattern. Tie on a large attractor pattern such as a Size 12 or 14 Patriot as the lead fly, and tie an ant or beetle about one to two feet behind it. You'll readily detect the attractor and more likely know the approximate location of the terrestrial floating behind it. You can also purposely sink the terrestrial by adding weight. Trout often feed on submerged terrestrials.

TYING TERRESTRIALS

Do you have trouble following your ant or beetle pattern on the surface? I've suggested earlier that terrestrials are often not easy to detect. I've also suggested ways to overcome this.

But you'll find other problems when you tie and use terrestrial patterns. Many tiers use deer to tie terrestrials. After catching a few trout, however, the deer hair splits. Deer hair can also be difficult to tie with. That's where some of the new synthetics come in. It's much easier to tie many of the terrestrials with some of these materials. One particular substance that many tiers use is Polycelon. This pliable material has made deer-hair ant, beetle, hopper, caterpillar, and cricket patterns outmoded. Just tie on one of the cylinders for an ant, beetle, grasshopper, cricket, or caterpillar, and you have an excellent imitation of this terrestrial. But you'll encounter another problem if you use some of these new synthetics: How the devil do you fasten them to the hook? Some of the new adhesives really help. Look at the Chernobyl Cricket later in this chapter as an example.

Don't overlook twisted terrestrials. Mike O'Brien uses twisted poly yarn for duns, spinners, and terrestrials. He substitutes poly yarn for Polycelon as body material for hoppers and crickets. Try tying some terrestrials with this method. See Chapter 6 for instructions.

THE PLASTIC BEETLE—POLY OR FOAM

You can tie beetle patterns with deer hair, foam, poly yarn, or a myriad of other synthetics that have recently come on the market. One of the easiest and most realistic-looking patterns is the Poly or Foam Beetle, and it goes with my philosophy of tying: Keep it simple. I often tie a belly of peacock, and then tie in the poly-yarn back. To help alleviate the problem of following this pattern, I tie in a piece of fluorescent orange or red poly yarn on top of the black back to make it much easier to see on the surface.

But sinking terrestrial patterns is also effective. Substitute black wool yarn for the poly and a wet-fly hook, and you have a beetle pattern that will sink quickly. To make it sink even faster, add a couple of wraps of weight to the body.

I usually try this pattern in midsummer and often on smaller streams. I'll never forget that trip with Ken Helfrich of Springfield, Oregon. Ken's probably the best guide I've ever had; he knows the Snake

River in Idaho and the McKenzie River in Oregon as well as any other guide. Ken spent a whole week with me while I wrote *Fishing Small Streams with a Fly Rod*. We fished just about every worthwhile tributary of the McKenzie River that week, and we caught plenty of trout. One of our prime patterns the entire week was the Poly Beetle.

I've suggested earlier that I often use a tandem rig when I fish. I tie on a Patriot as a strike indicator whether I use the beetle as a wet or dry fly.

Try this simple, easy-to-follow terrestrial pattern if you're looking for one that is lifelike and quick to tie.

Dressing: Plastic Beetle
Hook: Size 14 to 20 dry-fly hook.
Thread: Black.
Body (belly): Peacock.
Body (top): Black poly yarn or black foam.

1. Tie in black tying thread and wind back slightly beyond the bend of the hook.
2. Tie in a piece of black poly yarn about the size of a wooden matchstick (for a Size 14 or 16, larger for larger beetles) or a piece of black foam. If you use black foam, shape it so you can tie in a narrower piece. Cut the foam so the point where you tie it in is shaped like a "V."
3. Tie in a herl of peacock at the same point (at the bend) and wind it forward to the eye. Make certain that you have the thread at the eye before you wind the peacock.

4. *Now bring the poly over the top and tie in at the eye of the hook.* **This will produce a perfect beetle-like body. Note: If you want the Beetle pattern to sink quickly, substitute wool yarn for the poly.**

5. Tie off and clip the poly, leaving a short section to copy the head. *If you use foam, try this little trick showed to me by Garry Hitterman: Pull on the end of the foam before you cut the excess. Cut it so you have just a fraction of an inch in front.* **When you pull on the foam in this manner it will give you a curved head.**

6. *Whip-finish.*

7. *Add a drop of orange paint or orange yarn on the top back of the Beetle so it will be easier to detect. On some I put a bright color on the entire back.*

THE ELK HOP

Garry Hitterman of Casa Grande, Arizona, has tied great flies for more than thirty years. He has taught fly-tying classes and tied flies professionally for many of those years. He has tied thousands of dozens of flies and has taught me a lot about fly tying. He's an innovative fly tier in the true sense. In those thirty years of tying, Garry has created many new in-

Garry Hitterman of Casa Grande, Arizona, ties his great terrestrial pattern, the Elk Hop.

novative and productive trout patterns. He's especially creative when it comes to midge and terrestrial patterns. Garry fishes southwestern lakes and rivers frequently and has seen some fantastic trout feeding frenzies. He's seen terrestrials, especially grasshoppers, create some feeding events with trout in mid and late summer.

Garry has created a pattern he calls the Elk Hop. It's tied a lot like the Simple Salmon (Chapter 7). Like the Simple Salmon, the Elk Hop has several individual wings tied in as you progress up the shank toward the eye. But Garry goes one step further on this pattern—he tapers the body as he goes forward. When tying the Elk Hop, Garry ties in three separate bodies and four sets of wings. Each part of the body gets a bit more bulky as you move forward.

One of the biggest problems many tiers have is crowding the hook eye. Garry ties in the thread about one-fourth of the way back from the eye to remind him not to crowd it.

Dressing: Elk Hop
Hook: 2XL Size 10 dry-fly hook.
Thread: Yellow 6/0.
Body: Cahill-colored poly dubbing.
Wings: Rear three are regular elk
    hair and the front wings are
    bleached elk hair.

1. Start tying the thread in about one-quarter of the way back on the shank. *Garry does this to prevent crowding the eye.*
2. Tie in about a matchstick diameter of elk hair at the rear. Although it looks like the tail, this is the first wing. Cut the butts off close and at an angle so you can tie over them. In front of the wing, dub some cahill poly and wind forward a little less than half an inch. Tie in the second wing, again about the size of a matchstick. *Dub a bit more poly and wind forward again slightly less than a half-inch and tie in another wing.* **This procedure tapers the body as you move forward.**
3. *Note: Rather than cut the butts on the third wing, separate them to the right and left and tie in as legs (similar to the Hendrickson Emerger in Chapter 2).*
4. Continue the procedure with a bit more poly than last time, end up with a fourth wing in front, and clip the final butt section of the elk to form a head.
5. Tie off and whip-finish.

THE CHERNOBYL CRICKET

Someone gives me a pattern or two to try at just about every fly-fishing show I attend. Several years ago an angler gave me a big, gaudy cricket pattern. I placed it in my fly box and didn't look at it for three years. Then one day, on an old gold-dredging pond in Montana, I decided to give that terrestrial a try. Who gave it to me? What gave me the idea to use that particular dry fly under these very frustrating circumstances? I couldn't answer any of these questions as I hauled out the seventh trout I had caught in less than an hour. This last one, a heavy stream-bred brown trout, measured twenty-four inches long and probably hadn't seen a pattern like that before.

My son, Bryan, and Ken Rictor also fished nearby, but neither had much success with the grasshopper patterns they used. Why? The three of us sat back on the bank overlooking this dredge pond and studied our gear. Bryan and Ken both used a hopper pattern that should have worked reasonably well at that time and under those conditions. I, however, used a large black terrestrial pattern Ken immediately dubbed the Chernobyl Cricket. That huge black pattern saved the day.

I had only one of these big cricket patterns with me so I handed the fly rod—with the tattered pattern still attached—to Bryan and asked him to cast to a group of bushes on the far shore. His first cast landed within a couple inches of an overhanging branch. The cricket lay motionless for a couple seconds, and then Bryan began twitching the pattern. Seconds later we saw a huge dark shadow follow the terrestrial, inhale it, and the fight was on. In a few minutes Bryan landed and released an eighteen-inch brown trout.

Over the next hour Bryan landed seven more trout with that huge cricket pattern—most of them just shortly after he began twitching the fly. That cricket saved the day, changing it from a frustrating to a highly successful one. That solitary cricket pattern showed the wear and tear of the mouths of more than twenty huge trout.

Forget what you've been told before about dry flies and drag-free floats. Twitch this pattern when you fish it on slowly moving or still water. If that doesn't work, then try fishing it drag free. The more Bryan and I imparted motion to this huge cricket, the more vicious the strikes from the trout. The black rubber legs give even more motion when you move the pattern. I especially like to cast this fly in slow pools and under brush and bushes along the shore.

While fishing the cricket that afternoon, Ken, Bryan and I found one other interesting and important difference. While the two of them used conventional 5X tippet material, I used a two-and-a-half-foot piece of the new 5X fluorocarbon as my tippet. I added a piece of this tippet material to Ken's leader and he began catching trout on the grasshopper pattern that failed him before. I firmly believe, especially on still or nearly still water, that this new material is almost invisible to trout. After that afternoon of fishing on the dredge ponds, all three of us stopped at a local fly shop and bought a couple of spools of fluorocarbon—the experience that afternoon made believers out of all of us.

You'll find that this cricket pattern is relatively easy to tie. I use a one-inch-long piece of medium-diameter (about three-sixteenths-inch) black Polycelon cylinder. This material looks like cork but it is flexible. I cut the back end off at an angle so that when placed on the hook the upper end of the back is longer than the lower end. I use a razor blade to slit the bottom of the black poly so it slides over the Size 10 hook (Mustad 94831). I place a few drops of superglue on the hook and slide the body over top. (Watch the glue—I had a difficult time loosening my finger from one of the flies because I came in contact with it.) I let the glue set for a short time so the body fits snugly on the hook. I then turn the body upside down and apply another drop or two of glue to the cut area. I tie in the black tying thread and add the black rubber legs underneath, the deer hair (natural or black), and smolt blue Krystal Flash on top. Finally, I add a piece of bright orange or red poly yarn on top to help me locate the pattern on the water. That's it—it's that simple. I usually tie a dozen or two at a time like a production line.

What pattern will I faithfully use in late summer when no hatch appears? You guessed correctly—the Chernobyl Cricket. Don't ever go on any summer fishing trip without a good supply of these large, productive terrestrials. Ask Ken Rictor or Bryan Meck if they agree. They'll tell you how well this terrestrial pattern works!

Dressing: Chernobyl Cricket
Hook: Mustad 94831, Size 10 or 12.
Thread: Black.

Body: Black Polycelon cylinder (³⁄₁₆ inch in diameter and one inch long).
Back (thorax area): Smolt blue Krystal Flash, orange poly, and deer hair
(about twelve pieces).
Legs: Black rubber legs.

1. Make a cut in the Polycelon so it fits over the hook shank. Make certain
   it's a bit longer than the shank. Remember, the top rear should be a bit
   longer than the bottom. Use a single-edged razor, but cut very carefully.
2. *Make certain that the body has a slit along its entire length (or at least
   that part that fits on the shank). Place a drop of superglue on the shank
   and on the cut part of the body. (Don't touch the glue!) I often use a
   clothespin or two to hold the
   Polycelon on the hook until the
   glue dries. I then turn the body
   upside down and place more
   superglue on the slit.*

3. Make several turns with the
   black tying thread about one-
   eighth of an inch back from the
   front of the Polycelon.
4. Add the rubber legs underneath
   and the deer hair, Krystal Flash,
   and orange poly yarn on top.

5. Whip-finish and cement on top
   of the tying thread.

THE SUNKEN ANT

What a great late-August trip! There was no hatch, but there were lots of
ants on the water. The black ant pattern I used caught plenty of trout on
that hot, late summer afternoon.

But you don't have to wait until late summer to fish an ant pattern,
and you'll find that colors other than black will often produce more

strikes. If you look at some of the winged ants on the surface you'll see that some of them have a definite rusty brown tinge to their bodies. I've also found both wet and floating Cinnamon Ant patterns are effective.

Several years ago, Steve Snyder of Harrisburg, Pennsylvania, gave me some of his Cinnamon Ant patterns. They work well and are buoyant. Steve has a unique method of tying his ant. He dubs a small amount of fine cinnamon or rusty poly, and then moves the dubbed thread above the hook. He then pushes or slides the dubbing down along the thread to the hook. Steve winds in front of the hump, behind it, and a couple turns of thread around it. He does the same thing for the front hump of the body. Steve adds a few turns of brown hackle between the two parts or winds the hackle parachute-style around the front hump.

On many occasions I opt for the Cinnamon Ant when I fish terrestrials. This pattern also works well when the winged ant appears in late summer.

How do you fish your ant patterns? When the winged ant appears, I often use a three-foot-long 5X or 6X tippet. On occasions when I become frustrated with the selectivity of the trout feeding on these terrestrials, I head upstream and fish riffles and the heads of pools with a sinking ant pattern. Yes, a sinking ant pattern! I find that sinking ants, both black and cinnamon, work well—hatch or no hatch. Why? As I've often said with the Trico spinner fall, ants, once they are on the surface, can't escape and eventually sink. A sunken ant pattern works well and often produces when a floating pattern won't.

For the sunken black ant I often use a black bead to copy the front hump and dub in black angora for the back hump. The bead ensures that the pattern will sink, but I often add additional weight to the body and shove it up under the bead. I add seven wraps of .005- or .010-inch lead wire. If you plan to fish faster water, this heavier pattern gets deeper faster. I tie in a black soft hackle between the two parts of the body to copy the legs.

Chuck Robbins, a well-known Montana outdoor writer, introduced me to the Sunken Cinnamon Ant. He uses a copper bead for the front hump and dubs cinnamon angora for the back part. He uses a brown hackle in the middle to copy the legs. I've used Chuck's pattern on many occasions and it produces throughout the summer.

At best, ant patterns are difficult to follow on the surface. You can do several things when you're using them to help detect even the most subtle strikes. The late Russ Mowry, a noted fly tier from Latrobe, Pennsylvania, added a white post to his floating ant patterns so they were easier to detect on the surface. I said earlier that I sometimes tie a floating terrestrial behind a large dry fly like the Patriot. If you can see the large, Size 12 Patriot, then you can approximate where the ant pattern is. With the sunken ant, if the Patriot sinks you have a strike on the wet fly. I vary the distance between the two patterns from one to three feet depending upon the type and depth of the water.

Have you tried terrestrials this past year? What about ants? You might be staying away from them because they're so difficult to follow on the surface. Try using them in a tandem setup.

Dressing: Sunken Cinnamon Ant
Hook: Mustad 80200BR, Size 16.
Bead: Copper, size ⁷⁄₃₂ inch.
Thread: Rusty brown 6/0.
Body: Rusty angora (rear hump).
Hackle: One or two wraps of brown
    hackle.

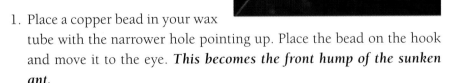

1. Place a copper bead in your wax
    tube with the narrower hole pointing up. Place the bead on the hook and move it to the eye. **This becomes the front hump of the sunken ant.**

2. *Dub rusty angora and make a hump in the rear. Try the method that Steve Snyder uses: Dub a small amount of the tying thread with rusty angora, or if you plan to fish the pattern dry use poly. Hold the tying thread above the hook and push all the material down to the rear part of the hook (for the rear hump). Wind around, then in front and in back of the hump.*

3. Tie in a brown hackle and make a couple of turns.
4. Whip-finish and cement.

THE WINGED ANT

For more than thirty-five years I've kept a log of every fishing trip I've taken. In that book I record the date, where I fished, what patterns I used, how effective these patterns were, and what hatches I saw. Look at three of the entries in my notes: August 26, 1988, on Big Fishing Creek; August 27, 1978, on Bowman Creek; and September 15, 1998, on the Little Juniata River—all in central and northeastern Pennsylvania. For those three dates I listed the winged ant as the predominant insect on the water. Depending on your preparation, that hatch—the winged ant—can be one of the most rewarding or most frustrating. Over those thirty-five years this terrestrial hatch appeared on the water around August 25, plus or minus five days.

After more than thirty years of fishing when winged ants were on the water, I can fairly easily discern trout rising to this hatch. It's often a subtle lethargic rise—definitely not a splashing one. It's a different type of rise form—trout often gently sip in the ants.

Tie this ant pattern in several sizes. I've seen some naturals as large as a Size 18 and others as small as a Size 22. Use dark blackish-brown poly dubbing to tie the two humps to imitate the body of the ant. I make the rear hump a bit larger than the front one. Tie the hackle in between the two humps.

The white poly-yarn wing on the Winged Ant makes the pattern more easily detectable under most conditions. When tying the pattern, tie the wing material as you would for a Quill Gordon or Hendrickson wet fly. Place the wing back over the two humps in a loop. Use a white hen hackle as the wing if you plan to sink the pattern. Include a dark brown hackle and tie it in between the two humps of the body. As I said earlier, add a bead if you want some of your patterns to sink quickly. Use the bead as the front hump. You can use a permanent marking pen and color the bead a dark brown.

Do you plan to fish Eastern or Midwestern trout waters in late summer or early fall? If you encounter a warm afternoon, look for those tell-tale rises that tell you winged ants are on the surface. Tie the pattern I've recommended in several sizes and get ready for some late-season action. The winged ant could be one of the last great trout feeding episodes of the year.

Dressing: Winged Ant
Hook: Size 18 to 22 dry-fly hook.
Thread: Dark brown 8/0.
Body: Dark brown fine poly dubbing.
Wings: White poly yarn (white hen hackle for a wet fly).
Hackle: black.

1. Wind dark brown tying thread back to the bend of the hook.
2. Dub dark brown poly and place four or five turns near the bend to make a hump. Or, follow the procedure for the Cinnamon Ant (step 2).
3. Tie in a black hackle just in front of the rear hump. Make three or four turns of hackle and tie off.
4. Dub dark brown poly and make about three turns to form a second hump in front of the hackle.
5. *Tie in a bunch (about half the size of a match stick) of white poly yarn at the eye to copy the wing. Loop the poly and tie in the other end. Have the loop extend back toward the back hump, but don't extend it too far. Tie off and cut the butts of the poly.*
6. Whip-finish and lacquer the head.

THE DEERHAIR OR POLY ANT

I like working with deer hair. I said earlier, however, that one of the problems with it is that it tends to split after catching a trout or two. That's why I began using the Poly Ant. Think of the Poly Ant as just a double Poly Beetle. With the Poly Beetle I tie in a piece of black poly yarn at the bend and bring it up and over the back. I do the same thing with the rear of the Poly Ant; then I repeat the process in the front to make the two humps.

Even though the deer hair splits, I've found that the worse it looks the more the trout seem to like it. The Deerhair Ant is one of those patterns that trout seem to like the shoddier it gets. It's extremely easy to tie and is lifelike. Try tying both patterns.

Dressing: Deerhair or Poly Ant
Hook: Mustad 94833, Size 14 to 20.
Thread: Black.
Body: Black deer hair or black poly yarn.
Hackle: Tips of the black deer hair or black hackle.

1. Tie in a bunch of black deer hair with the tips extending over the bend of the hook, or tie in a three-inch piece of black poly yarn.
2. *Wind the tying thread back over the deer or poly back to a point just beyond the bend. Move the thread to a point halfway up the shank. Cover the shank completely with the black thread.*
3. *Bring the deer hair or poly over top of the bend, make a hump for the rear half of the ant, tie in, and wind the thread halfway up the shank. Leave the tips of the deer hair for legs; move the hair to the right and left sides.*
4. *Tie in another equal bunch of deer hair or poly yarn and do the same you did with the last piece. This time, however, point the tips of the deer hair or poly out over the hook eye. Wind back to the center (just in front of the rear hump) and bring the deer hair or poly over the top and tie in. Leave the tips of the deer hair for additional legs if necessary. Tie a black hackle at the center if you're using poly.*
5. Tie off and cement.

You've learned to tie seven different terrestrials in Chapter 4. Each of these is especially productive on those hot summer days.

5

Conventional
Dry Flies

TECHNIQUES YOU WILL
LEARN IN THIS CHAPTER

1. An easy method of pushing the hackle back from the eye (Patriot, step 14)
2. A method for moving and securing troublesome divided wings (Patriot, step 5)
3. Another method for securing dry-fly wings (Patriot, step 6)
4. How to measure the correct wing length before you tie it on the shank (Patriot, step 3)
5. How to make certain you have the proper hackle length (Patriot, step 12)
6. How to wrap two hackles at the same time (Patriot, step 13)
7. How to make the tail fibers all of equal length (Patriot, step 8)
8. How to insure that the tails on a dry fly are the correct length (Patriot, step 9)

9. **How to prevent body material from slipping over the bend of the hook (Patriot, step 10)**
10. **How to make a tail, body, and wings from one continuous piece of material (Strike Indicator, steps 2 through 4)**
11. **How to make a dubbing loop the easy way (Hybrid, step 7)**
12. **How to add an egg sac to an imitation (Upright Spinner, step 6)**
13. **How to insure that hackle will be less cramped (Hybrid, step 8)**
14. **How to place wings properly with epoxy (Chocolate Dun, step 4)**

For more than thirty years dry flies reigned supreme for me. I relied on such well-known patterns as the Light Cahill, Dark Cahill, Adams, and dozens of other dry flies. All of these floating flies had two upright and divided wings. They also had two hackles wound behind and in front of those upright wings. Anglers call this type of dry fly the Catskill, classic, or high-riding dry fly. You'll tie this type of pattern in this chapter.

But there are other types of floating patterns. In addition to the Catskill type, you have the parachute dry fly with the hackle wound around the base of a single wing called the post. You'll find parachutes in a later chapter. Then you have Comparadun patterns where there is no hackle. The deer-hair wing is formed in a semicircle so that the right and left sides of the deer hair act as hackle and keep the fly afloat. There are many other types of dry flies that are hybrids or mixtures.

Do I still rely on dry flies? I just stated that I used dry flies almost exclusively for many years. I hated fishing wet flies in those years. I didn't consider myself a good wet-fly fisherman and depended almost entirely on dry flies. Besides, when I used floating patterns, I saw the action unfold in front of me on top of the surface in full view. I wrote about the joys of fishing dry flies in my first book, *Meeting and Fishing the Hatches*.

But a strange thing happened to me about a decade ago. I began to use wet flies and caught a lot more trout. Let's face it—trout feed much more often under the surface than they do on top. I now use wet flies in tandem setups with dry flies acting as strike indicators.

There are, however, many dry-fly patterns I still rely on, especially when I use the tandem. I have used the Patriot as a dry fly or strike indicator in a tandem setup for more than a decade. This pattern floats all day and readily alerts the angler when a trout has struck the wet fly in the tandem. I recently concocted a new attractor pattern I call the Strike Indicator. This bright orange poly dry fly looks a lot like a piece of poly yarn with a tail, hackle, and hook. Have you ever used a bright poly strike indicator and had a trout strike the indicator? The Strike Indicator is an attractor pattern with an attitude. If trout strike the indicator pattern they get hooked.

There are other dry-fly patterns that I feel are important. A pattern like the Hybrid has a special place in my fly box.

As you dress each pattern, you'll find some tying suggestions that might be new and unusual. Give each of the suggestions a fair trial. Keep them in your repertoire of tying techniques if you feel comfortable with them.

FISHING THE CONVENTIONAL PATTERNS

Of all the dry flies I use I enjoy fishing conventional patterns the most. Why? They float high and are usually easy to follow on the surface. I'll never forget that first day I spent on western trout waters if I live to be a hundred. That first morning, completely by myself, I saw a great hatch—albeit sparse—of western green drakes. I matched that hatch with a high-riding conventional Green Drake pattern. That fly saved the day—no, the trip—for me. That single high-riding Western Green Drake rode the snow-fed waters of Montana's Bitterroot River for two hours while duns appeared and trout fed on them. And it caught trout—and plenty of them. That same pattern worked well on the prolific Henry's Fork in eastern Idaho. Even though dozens of anglers crowded this spring-fed stream, the high-riding Western Green Drake caught heavy rainbow trout.

But I tie some unusual patterns in this chapter. The Patriot, Hybrid, and Strike Indicator are those special flies I use when no hatch appears.

These patterns seem to bring trout to the surface. I use these conventional patterns most often as the lead fly for a tandem rig. The Patriot and the Hybrid, with their upright, divided white calf-body wings become excellent "strike indicators." Using them as strike indicators gives you an added benefit: They also catch trout. I call these patterns strike indicators with an attitude.

TYING THE CONVENTIONAL PATTERNS

The patterns might be conventional, but many tiers encounter problems tying some of these and other dry flies. I've added a few twists to tying some of them to make your job easier and to make the patterns more durable. Who hasn't had trouble separating the wings of dry flies? Many tiers have trouble dividing the wings made from hair or feathers. I have also experienced this problem. If you've mastered the figure-eight method of placing wings, then you've overcome this obstacle. If you haven't mastered that tying technique, try the one I use for the Patriot. By using a piece of tying thread, you can easily separate the wings and be assured that they'll stay separated.

Other tiers complain that if they use synthetic materials for the body, these materials tend to slip over the bend of the hook after a few casts. Again, I've found a way to overcome this tying problem. Just leave one of the Krystal Flash strands behind at the hook bend when you wind the others forward. Bring the remaining strand up and over the others and tie it in. This will prevent the body material from slipping back over the bend.

Some tiers have problems getting the length of the tail correct and the fibers even. Just a simple trick will eliminate these two problems. To get the fibers equal, use your thumb and forefinger and stroke the hackle to make the fibers stand out straight. Next, grab about five to ten of the fibers and quickly move downward to strip them from the stem. You'll now have all the fibers of equal length. Place the hackle fibers on the shank at the bend of the hook and tie in. Make the tail very short initially, wrap around the butts two or three times, then pull the tail fibers out to the correct length. The tails should usually be about the length of the hook shank.

One other problem always seems to crop up when tying conventional patterns: placing the hackle on the shank correctly. I usually use two hackles to make a dry fly float better. But if you wind over the same general area of the hook, you'll cramp down some of the hackle previously wrapped. If you weave the hackle as you wind, you'll find the problem less bothersome. Step 8 in the Hybrid explains the process.

And there's another problem when it comes to hackle placement. Some of the hackle often crowds the hook eye. You can prevent this if you use a short-nozzled bobbin or a ballpoint pen. Step 14 in the Patriot will help you use this technique.

THE PATRIOT

Why include blue in a dry-fly pattern? A few decades ago, two Canadian professors conducted experiments with colors and how rainbow trout react to them. They found that trout often select a blue salmon egg before most other colors. Because of that study and an article in *Fly Fishing the West,* I decided to add blue to one of my patterns.

I tied my first Patriot back in 1985. I compared how effective that new attractor measured up to nineteen other well-known dry-fly patterns. Some of those other patterns were the Wulff Royal Coachman, Adams, Light Cahill, and Quill Gordon. I cast each one of twenty dry-fly patterns one thousand times on the same river in water where no trout rose. At no time did I cast over rising trout. I tied each of the twenty patterns on a Size 12 hook. In those tests, the Patriot caught almost two trout for every one caught on any of the other flies. Since those experiments, I have used the Patriot almost exclusively when no hatch appears, and often with exciting results.

The Patriot works well all across the United States. It's even produced plenty of trout in New Zealand. Of the thirteen largest trout Mike

Manfredo and I caught in that friendly island nation, twelve of them struck the Patriot. I've had glowing reports about the effectiveness of the Patriot across the United States, Chile, Argentina, and Bolivia. From Montana's top rivers to those in New Mexico, anglers have reported exciting results with the Patriot. One afternoon on the Minipi River system in Labrador, Steve McDonald and I caught a half-dozen big brook trout on a Size 10 Patriot. I'm certain we would have caught more but we lost our last pattern on a heavy fish.

One of the top attributes of the Patriot is its brilliant, easy-to-detect color scheme. With its white wings, it's easy to follow on the surface even in the heavy canopy so often present on small streams. That's why the pattern makes a good strike indicator when you use a tandem made up of a dry fly (the Patriot) and a wet fly.

Do other anglers feel the Patriot works for them? Orvis lists the pattern in its catalog and sold more than seven thousand Patriots the first year.

I've tied more than five thousand Patriots in the past fifteen years. I've given some of them out at workshops and seminars, and tied some for shadow boxes. While tying all of these patterns, I've found some simplified methods of executing several of the fly-tying steps. The techniques I've developed have made tying the pattern easier.

Dressing: Patriot

Hook: Mustad 94833, Size 10 to 18.

Thread: Fiery orange-red.

Tail: Brown hackle fibers.

Body: Smolt blue Krystal Flash wound around the shank with the red tying thread as a midrib (similar to the Royal Coachman).

Wings: White calf body hair.

Hackle: Brown.

1. Wind the tying thread about one-third of the way back on the shank of the hook.

2. Cut off about twenty to thirty hairs from a piece of white calf body and place them in a stacker to even the tips.

3. Tie in the hair near the butt section. *First, lay the stack of hair over the body to make certain it is the length of the hook shank.* Have the tips of the hair extending forward out over the eye of the hook. The butt or section you cut should extend toward the rear. Make several tight turns to hold the hair in place. The upright wings should be about as long as the hook shank.

4. Tie about ten to fifteen turns of thread in front of the hair to make them stand nearly erect. Take the tying thread and divide the hair in half. Do this by moving the tying thread through the middle of the hair. Make a figure-eight to divide the hair. Don't worry if the wings are exactly upright or if they're divided—the next step will help you do that. If you can't make a figure-eight, do the following:

5. *Tie in a six-inch piece of tying thread just behind the wings. (Or you can make a three-inch loop in your thread. Tie off the loop and cut one end close to the shank and you have a six-inch piece of thread.) Take that piece of thread and wind it around the left wing and tie it off with the regular tying thread. Now take that same piece of thread and wind it around the right wing and tie it off. Before you tie the thread off on each wing, adjust the wing just as you'd like it—then secure the thread. On some cantankerous wings you might have to make two complete turns.*

6. *Here's an alternate method with less troublesome wings: Take a six-inch piece of tying thread and place the middle of it underneath the eye of the hook. Take both ends of this short tying thread and place them between the two wings. Tie in the two pieces just behind the wing.*

7. Wind the tying thread back to the bend of the hook.

8. *Take a brown spade hackle and stroke the fibers so they stand out from the stem. Take a half-dozen of the fibers and pinch them between the thumb and forefinger. Quickly move the fingers in a downward movement and the fibers will come free from the stem.* **This method guarantees that all tail fibers will be even.**

9. *The tail fibers should be about as long as the shank of the hook (on a normal dry-fly hook). Tie in the tail fibers shorter than they should be (less than the shank of the hook) and secure with three wraps of thread tied over the butt sections. Now pull the tails out to the correct length. Now secure the tail with a half-dozen wraps of thread.*

10. *Take five strands of smolt blue Krystal Flash and tie them in at the bend of the hook. Leave one of these strands behind in a material clip. Take the other four strands and wind them up the shank about one-third of the way. Tie off but don't clip. Pull the remaining strand of Krystal Flash tightly over the other four and tie it off at the midsection. **This one last strand prevents the others from sliding down the bend of the hook.** Now make a midrib (midsection) with the tying thread.*

11. Don't cut the Krystal Flash. Wind the remainder just in front of the midsection up to the wing. Now cut off the excess.

12. Select two brown hackles (I often use one saddle hackle). Make certain that they are a matched pair (equal in width and length). *You can see if they are the correct width by bending them and comparing their width with the wing length. The hackle barbules should be slightly shorter than the wing.* Place the dull sides of the two hackles facing forward (the underside as you look at the neck).

13. Wind one hackle and then the other first behind and then in front of the wings. I usually make about 60 to 70 percent of the wraps behind the wing, and 30 to 40 percent in front of the wings. Tie off just behind the eye. *(Optional: You can tie the two hackles at the same time. Grab them with a hackle pliers and wind them both at one time. Make certain that you have equal tension on both.)*

14. *Whip-finish with a pen or with the bobbin.*

THE STRIKE INDICATOR

Do you ever use a strike indicator? Have you ever had a trout strike at that indicator? If you've fished a brightly colored indicator long enough, you've probably seen trout hit it. I've had the same frustrating experience many times. What can you do? Add a hook to bright orange material and call it the Strike Indicator. Is the Strike Indicator easy to follow? You bet it is. Does it float in full view? Yes it does! But the ultimate question looms: Does the pattern catch trout?

I first used the Strike Indicator in a fit of frustration. That first time I used it with a Zebra Midge and caught a half-dozen trout on the dry fly. Soon an angler nearby bellowed out to me, "What the devil are you using?"

"A Strike Indicator," I yelled back.

"No. What fly did you catch those trout on?" he asked.

"A Strike Indicator."

This banter went back and forth for several minutes before he came over to me and I showed him the Strike Indicator pattern.

"Now I see why you called it the Strike Indicator," he said after he saw the bright orange color of the pattern.

The Strike Indicator is easy to locate even under low-light conditions. It also floats well even if you use a wet fly with weight. I use Glo Bug material for the tail, body, and wings. Have you ever noticed how long it takes for this material to sink? The Glo Bug material seems to float forever.

Dressing: Strike Indicator

Hook: Mustad 94833, Size 10 to 18.

Thread: Fluorescent orange-red.

Tail: Fluorescent orange Glo Bug material tied in like a shuck.

Body: Fluorescent orange Glo Bug material wound around the shank.

Wings: Fluorescent orange Glo Bug material, divided.

Hackle: Bright orange.

1. Tie in the tying thread and wind it back to the bend of the hook.
2. *Take a six-inch piece of the fluorescent orange Glo Bug material and tie it in. This will become the tail, body, and wings.*

3. *Extend the orange Glo Bug material about the length of the hook shank be-yond the bend.* **This bright orange tail imitates a nymphal shuck.**

4. *Now wrap the remainder of the orange Glo Bug material around the shank and up to just behind the eye of the hook. Don't cut the remainder off—you'll use that for the wing.*

5. *Make several turns of thread in front of the wing to make it stand erect, then divide the wings with the thread. Wind around the base of each wing with the thread in a figure-eight (or use the method discussed in the Patriot, step 5). The wings should be about as long as the shank of the hook—cut the excess if they are too long.*

6. *Tie in two bright orange hackles just behind the wing. Try wrapping the two at the same time. Grab the two hackle tips and make certain that they are equally tight and start winding both at the same time.*

7. Whip-finish.

THE HYBRID

I've seen plenty of new patterns in my lifetime. With the advent of many new fly tiers in recent years has come a proliferation of new patterns. I too am always experimenting with new patterns, continuously looking for that ultimate pattern. I'm always dreaming of that fly that catches every trout I see. I recently searched for a pattern that would copy some of the darker hatches and still be easy to see. Here is how I came up with a new, effective pattern I dubbed the Hybrid.

What's one of the most common body colors that trout see all season long? If you've read *The Hatches Made Simple,* then you know it's got to be gray. In the spring, trout see blue quills, black quills, quill Gordons, and hendricksons. All of these have gray or dark brown as part of their body colors. And slate drakes, blue quills, and others with dark gray bodies appear on North American waters in late May, June, and July and again in September and October. What can you use to match the slate drake? Again, a dark gray pattern works well. That's why the Adams, Gray Wulff, and even the Ausable Wulff, with its brown to dark brown body, are effective patterns much of the year.

I, however, have difficulty following the Adams and Gray Wulff on the surface. I can't locate the gray or brown wings of these patterns quickly. Furthermore, I most often use the dry fly as the lead fly in the tandem rig (using the dry fly as a strike indicator and a wet fly behind that). If you use the tandem, it's mandatory that you can see and follow the dry fly closely. If you've used the Adams, Gray Wulff, or Slate Drake, you already know that they are not easy to follow. What can you do? Substitute white wings to make the pattern much more noticeable on the surface. Those white wings make all the difference in the world.

Why is this new pattern called the Hybrid? Compare the Adams, Gray Wulff, and Ausable Wulff with the Hybrid. The Hybrid includes two of the four basic parts of each of them. That's why I call the pattern the Hybrid. What I did was select the best from the best. The white calf wings of the Ausable Wulff give the pattern high visibility. The deer-hair tail from the Gray Wulff makes the pattern float well. The grizzly and brown hackle from the Adams and Gray Wulff makes the Hybrid ride high. The gray body of the Adams and Gray Wulff copies many of the great hatches of the season. So, in theory, the Hybrid should catch trout.

But the ultimate question about the Hybrid was, Does the new pattern work?

I tried the Hybrid on the ultimate frustrating river—the Delaware. Over the years I've found this particular water, especially when no hatch appears, to be one of the most baffling rivers that I have ever fished. I've left that river several times swearing that I'd never come back—but I always do.

In September the Delaware hosts a great slate drake hatch. It's one of the last large hatches of the season on that river. That was an ideal time to test the Hybrid pattern. One late afternoon in September several years ago, I caught three heavy trout on that dry-fly pattern. I caught several more on the beadhead Pheasant-Tail Nymph point fly. That might not seem like a lot of trout but it was to me—especially on the Delaware. As I scanned the surface, I saw an occasional trout feed on one of the emerging slate drakes that didn't make it to an exposed rock. I finally tore the wet fly off and cast

Table 2. Tying recipes for the Adams, Ausable Wulff, Gray Wulff, and Hybrid. Those listed in bold are part of the Hybrid.

PATTERN	WING	TAIL	BODY	HACKLE
Adams	Grizzly hackle tips	Brown and grizzly hackle fibers	**Medium gray poly**	**Grizzly and brown, mixed**
Ausable Wulff	**White calf, divided**	Moose	Brown opossum	**Grizzly and brown, mixed**
Gray Wulff	Brown deer hair	**Brown deer hair**	**Medium gray poly**	Medium gray
Hybrid	White calf, divided	Brown deer hair	Medium gray poly	Grizzly and brown, mixed

over some of the risers with the Hybrid, and three more of those difficult trout took the pattern that afternoon.

But the pattern showed its true colors on a trip to New York's Beaverkill in late April. That hallowed water holds the entire roster of early-season mayfly hatches, and a Size 14 Hybrid dry fly worked well when a hendrickson hatch appeared.

Do you want to try a great pattern that is highly visible, floats well, works much of the season—and above all catches trout? Then try the Hybrid—it's got everything to make it an effective pattern.

Tie the pattern in Sizes 12 to 18. You can use some of the smaller patterns to match the blue quill hatches common much of the year. I like to use an extra-light hook to tie the Hybrid. That lighter hook makes this dry-fly float even higher. Try this pattern, especially when some of the dark gray hatches appear. It might be the fly for which you've been searching.

Dressing: Hybrid

Hook: Use a hook like the Mustad 94833, Size 12 to 18.

Thread: Gray.

Tail: Tan deer hair.

Body: Medium to dark gray poly, dubbed.

Wings: White calf-body hair.

Hackle: One brown and one grizzly hackle.

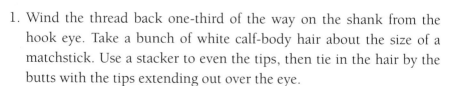

1. Wind the thread back one-third of the way on the shank from the hook eye. Take a bunch of white calf-body hair about the size of a matchstick. Use a stacker to even the tips, then tie in the hair by the butts with the tips extending out over the eye.
2. Make several turns over the butt section to hold the hair in place. The upright wings should be about as long as the shank of the hook.
3. Tie about ten to fifteen turns of thread in front of the hairs to make them stand nearly erect. Then take the tying thread and divide the

hair in half. Do this by moving the tying thread through the middle of the bunch. Make a figure-eight to divide the hair.

4. Tie in a six-inch piece of tying thread just behind the wings. Take that piece of thread and wind it around the left wing and tie it off with the regular tying thread. Now take that same piece of thread and wind it around the right wing and tie it off. Before you tie the thread off on each wing, adjust the wing just as you'd like it, then secure the thread.

5. Alternate method with less troublesome wings: Place the middle of a six-inch piece of tying thread underneath the eye of the hook. Take both ends of this short tying thread and place them between the two wings. Tie in the two pieces just behind the wing.

6. Take a half-dozen brown deer-body hairs and tie them in at the bend of the hook. Pull down tightly on the hairs to spread them. Make several looser wraps to make them stay in place.

7. *Dub in dark gray poly. Do it this way: First make a loop in your tying thread. Tie off the looped part from the rest of the tying thread. Place the dubbing fairly evenly in the loop from top to bottom. Take your hackle pliers and connect it to the bottom of the loop. Spin the loop until it's tight. Wind the poly over the body toward the wing.*

8. Tie in one brown and one grizzly hackle in back of the wing. Both hackles should have the dull side facing forward. Tie in the brown hackle first. Make about five turns behind the wing and three in front, then tie off. Now take the grizzly hackle and wind in the same manner. *Take your time with the second hackle and weave it over the first.* **By moving the second hackle slowly back and forth as you wind it over the first one, you're able to have more hackle stand upright.** Tie off the second hackle.

9. Finish the head and whip-finish.

THE UPRIGHT SPINNER

How many times have I been frustrated with the pale morning dun and sulphur hatches? I can't count the number of times—there's way too many of them. You'll find the pale morning dun very common on most trout rivers of the West, including those of Alaska. The sulphur is common on many Eastern and Midwestern waters. One of the inherent problems with these hatches is that often the duns emerge and the spinners fall onto the surface concurrently. Often at dusk, I thought I was prepared with the Sulphur Dun pattern tied on my tippet, but the sulphur spinner fall was the dominant food and trout fed on the latter. I've often sworn that I'd take two fly rods with me on those evenings—one with a Sulphur Spinner and the other with a Sulphur Dun. The sulphur most often appears at dusk, and you spend precious time fumbling, changing patterns in the half-light.

If you've fished this hatch and spinner fall very often, you already know that some of the spinners don't fall spent but rather sit upright for a while. How do you copy that spinner?

There is a solution to the problem—the Upright Spinner. The pattern has the general coloration of the female spinner, with upright wings rather than spent ones. With its tan body, trout taking the sulphur dun or spinner will often take the Upright Spinner imitation.

Dressing: Upright Spinner (Sulphur and Pale Morning Spinner)
Hook: Mustad 94833, Size 14 to 18.
Thread: Tan.
Tail: Tan deer hair.
Body: Tan poly, dubbed.
Wings: White poly yarn, divided.
Hackle: Tan, clipped on the bottom.

1. Wind tan thread back one-third of the way on the shank from the eye of the hook. *Take a two-inch piece of white poly yarn and tie in, then tie in the poly by the butts with the tips extending out over the eye.*
2. *Make several turns over the poly to hold it in place.*
3. *Tie about ten to fifteen turns of thread in front of the poly to make it stand nearly erect. Then take the tying thread and divide the poly in half. Do this by moving the tying thread through the middle of the poly. Make a figure-eight to divide the poly. Don't worry if the wings are exactly upright or if they're divided—the next step will help you with that.*

4. *Alternate method with less troublesome wings: Place the middle of a six-inch piece of tying thread underneath the eye of the hook. Take both ends of this short tying thread and place them between the two wings. Tie in the two pieces just behind the wing.*

5. Take a half-dozen brown deer-body hairs for the tail and tie them in at the bend of the hook. *Pull down tightly on the hairs to spread them. Then make several looser wraps to make them stay in place.*

6. *You can now dub some orange poly onto the thread and make two turns with that just in front of the tail.* **This represents the egg sac.** *Alternate method: Tie in the egg sac by dubbing orange poly before you tie in the tail. On this second method you tie in the egg sac on the upper end of the hook bend.*

7. *Dub in tan poly. Do it this way: First make a loop in your tying thread. Place wax on the loop. Then place the dubbing fairly evenly in the loop from top to bottom. With the hackle pliers, spin the loop until it's tight. Wind the poly over the body toward the wing.*

8. Tie in the tan hackle with the dull side facing forward. Make about five turns behind the wing and three in front; then tie off. *Take your time with the second hackle and weave it over the first.* Tie off the second hackle.

9. Finish the head and whip-finish.

THE CHOCOLATE DUN

The great hatches of late May and early June often mask the lesser-known ones. What do I mean? Have you ever fished a large drake hatch like the green drake and ended up catching trout on a Sulphur dun or spinner pattern? The same thing goes with the chocolate dun. Be prepared with a Size 16 pattern if you see trout feeding on small dark duns in the middle of the day.

Where have I seen some of the heaviest hatches of chocolate duns? The Delaware River and Beaverkill in New York hold good populations, as do central Pennsylvania trout streams like Pine and Big Fishing Creeks. Small fertile streams often harbor surprisingly good numbers.

The chocolate dun is fairly easy to identify. Look for the chocolate brown body, medium gray wings, gray tail, and creamish-tan legs. Tie the dun and spinner on a Size 16 Mustad 94833 hook.

But wait! There's a bonus: This same Chocolate Dun pattern in the same size copies other hatches. One of these (the male of *Ephemerella needhami*) appears on many waters of the Northeast on evenings in mid-June. That gives you a second opportunity to match a hatch with the same pattern a bit later in the season.

If you happen to fish in the early afternoon or evening in late May or early June—even into mid and late June—and you see trout rising, you might assume that they are rising to the March brown, blue quill, or another of the more famous hatches. Look again; they might be rising to a small dark brown mayfly that gets no attention and no respect. Those trout just might be rising to a hatch of the little-known but sometimes highly important chocolate duns.

Dressing: Chocolate Dun
Hook: Mustad 94833, Size 16.
Thread: Dark brown 8/0.
Tail: Pale gray hackle fibers.
Body: Chocolate brown poly dubbing.
Wings: Medium gray hen hackle tips.
Hackle: Creamish-tan hackle.

1. Tie in the tying thread just behind the eye. Make a couple of turns to secure.
2. Get two hen hackles and use a wing burner to get the proper shape and size. Place the outer sides of the hackles back-to-back and tie them in with the tips extending out over the eye. Now make several wraps di-rectly in front of the wings so they stand erect.

3. Take a six-inch piece of tying thread and make a harness. Take the loop of the thread under the eye and bring the two loose ends between the wings and tie them off immediately behind the wings.

4. *Place a drop of epoxy on the tied-in butts of the wings and let it set for a couple of minutes. Move and hold the wings until the glue holds them firmly in the position you want. The wings should now be set permanently with the epoxy.*

5. Wind the thread back to the bend of the hook. Grasp a large dun hackle with the thumb and forefinger. Stroke the fibers on the hackle stem until they are at a 45-degree angle and then pull a half-dozen downward until they are unattached. Tie in short and pull the fibers out to length. They should be as long as the shank of the hook.

6. Dub the chocolate brown poly and wind forward on the body to the wing.

7. Tie in a tan hackle and make five to seven turns behind and in front of the wing.

8. Whip-finish.

By now you've probably learned a few new tricks to add to your repertoire when tying flies. Try them out, keep tying the patterns, and use those innovative techniques you few comfortable with—discard those with which you're not comfortable. You've also learned to tie a few new highly effective patterns such as the Patriot, Strike Indicator, Hybrid, and Upright Spinner.

6

Spentwings

1. How to split the tails of a spinner (Red Quill Spinner, step 3)
2. A second way to split the tails of a spinner (Red Quill Spinner, step 4)
3. How to make perfect spent wings from a hackle (Twisted Coffin Fly Spinner, step 5, and Twisted Green Drake Spinner, step 5)
4. A second method of making spent wings from a large hackle (Twisted Coffin Fly Spinner, step 5, and Twisted Green Drake Spinner, step 5)
5. How to add weight and use heavier materials on a spinner pattern to make it sink beneath the surface (Weighted Female Trico Spinner, step 1)
6. Using a special material for spinner wings (Red Quill Spinner, step 6)
7. How to tie an upright spinner (Pale Morning Sulphur Spinner, step 4)

8. Making marks on the sides of some of the Drake patterns (Twisted Green Drake Spinner, step 2; also see Chapter 8—Twisted Brown Drake, step 3)
9. How to add a tail to a twisted spinner pattern (Twisted Coffin Fly Spinner, step 3)
10. How to add a short post to a spinner pattern so it's easier to follow (Twisted Coffin Fly Spinner, step 8)
11. How to add a parachute-type hackle to a spinner pattern (Twisted Coffin Fly Spinner, step 6)

Spinner patterns or "spent wings" make up an important part of your arsenal of imitations. They copy dead or dying adult mayflies—most often females that have laid their eggs. Spinners die on the surface with wings spread out or "spent." Spinners often fall in concentrated numbers, and with exceptions, like the Trico, pale morning dun, and dark brown spinner (*Paraleptophlebia*) and many of the early spring and some Western mayfly hatches, most spinner falls occur in the evening. If you plan to use one of these patterns, the most propitious time is often at dusk. In *The Hatches Made Simple,* I said that you need only six spinner patterns to match the vast majority of spinner falls. Those patterns are the Cream Spinner, Dark Olive Spinner, Tan Spinner, Rusty Spinner, Dark Reddish Brown Spinner, and Black Spinner. We'll tie a white, a dark maroon, and a tan-bodied spinner in this chapter.

FISHING THE SPENTWINGS

Spinner falls begin early in the season. Fly fishers often don't take advantage of these early but extremely important spentwings. Anglers eagerly fly fish over April hatches like the little blue-winged olive dun, hendrickson, blue quill, and quill Gordon, but often overlook the potentially great spinner falls these same insects present. I've witnessed spectacular falls as early as mid-April with the red quill spinner (adult of the hendrickson) and dark brown spinner (adult of the early blue quill). In the

Southwest (Arizona and New Mexico), I've fished over heavy spinner falls in January and February.

I said earlier that during the summer you can expect to see most of the spinner falls at dusk. Not so with these early-season mating flights. Once the hendrickson or blue quill have emerged in numbers, you can estimate the spinner fall to occur in the afternoon a day or two later, depending on the weather.

It's not uncommon to see more than one spinner fall in progress on a stream, especially in late spring and early summer. On highly productive streams like the Beaverkill in New York, in May or June you can expect to see several different spinners falling at dusk. I've often switched patterns three or four times trying to keep up with what spentwings the trout are feeding on.

I've learned a lot about these mating adults in the past fifty years of fishing. In addition to recognizing that more than one spinner fall can occur at the same time and taking advantage of the early-season spentwings, there are several other important principles that you should follow for successful spinner fishing. When fishing a spinner pattern, a drag-fee float can mean the difference between having a great or a lousy day. I often think a drag-free float is even more important when you fish spinner patterns. Another important aspect is to attempt to match the color of the spinner as closely as possible.

How do you know when a spinner fall will occur? The more you know about the life cycle of the mayfly hatch you're fishing, the better prepared you'll be. Many duns that emerge sporadically reappear on the surface as spinners in unbelievable numbers. Many of us forget that many mayflies emerge sporadically throughout the day without the burst of activity we often associate with hatches. Blue-winged olives, gray foxes, and gray drakes emerge in a less-than-concentrated form. When the gray fox dun sheds its pellicle, anglers call it the ginger quill spinner. The female mates and returns to the surface to lay its eggs, usually just at sunset and a day or two after the dun emerged from the water. Not only do spinners concentrate their activity at dusk, but also they're often very predictable—you can meet the same spinner fall for several weeks with anticipated regularity.

Sinking Spinner Patterns

Sometimes it pays to try unorthodox methods when you fly fish: fishing a spinner pattern as a wet fly is one example. Often larger trout prefer staying on or near the bottom to feed rather than rising to the surface. After floating on the surface through a few riffles, why wouldn't spinners sink and be available underneath? Look at the Trico spinner. It falls in unbelievable numbers on some of our trout streams for more than three months. And since the spinner is so small, wouldn't trout expend more energy than they gain by rising to the surface for them? That's why you often see trout feeding in a predictable rhythm and taking several at one time. And that's why bouquet or cluster flies work so well during a Trico spinner fall.

None of this made sense until I fly fished on Falling Springs Branch in south-central Pennsylvania more than twenty years ago. I stood across from an elderly angler while the Trico spinner fall ensued. I tied on a Size 24 Female Trico Spinner, fished over several rising trout for more than a half-hour, and caught nothing—zilch. Now I don't mind getting shut out, but when someone near me does well while I'm not catching anything, I get frustrated. That fly fisher across from me caught and released a half-dozen trout while I hadn't had a strike! I became more frustrated with each trout this seasoned angler caught. Soon I stopped fishing completely and watched him land another heavy rainbow. Finally I had enough—I lost my timidity and pride and asked him what pattern he found so effective. Maybe he didn't hear me, but he didn't utter a word. I pleaded a second time asking him what he was using. Finally, about ten minutes later as he walked away, he muttered an answer to my question: "I'm sinking the Trico Spinner."

It makes sense. Think about it for a minute. What happens to the thousands of Trico spinners that fall to the surface of a stream? Do they all remain on the surface or do some of them sink underneath after floating through several sets of rapids? And what about feeding trout? Will many of the larger fish remain near the surface to take Tricos floating

overhead or will they stay nearer the bottom and take the spinners drift-
ing underneath? And sunken spinners are available to the trout well after
the fall on the surface has ended.

After I heard those words of wisdom from the old angler, I went
home and tied a dozen weighted Trico Spinner patterns. I added weight
to the bodies of the dry flies and placed them in a fly box where they re-
mained until a few years ago. You know the routine: Tie up a new pattern that you've heard about or you've seen catch trout, and then totally
forget about it. It stays in one of your compartmentalized boxes for years
and years—never used—but it's there in case of an emergency.

Would I ever use those weighted Tricos I tied up after that day on
Falling Springs? I was asked to give a talk and demonstration recently at Upper Canyon Outfitters near Alder, Montana. I arrived a day early at the lodge
on the Ruby River, so I had a chance to fish and acquaint myself with the
water. It happened on that early August morning that a fantastic Trico hatch
appeared. So many of these Tricos appeared in the air that they formed a
cloud just in front of me. I saw only a couple of trout surface for the spinners, but for more than an hour I cast over them without getting as much as
one strike. During that frustrating hour some of the registrants for tomorrow's seminar arrived and stopped by the river to watch me. Now the pressure was on: I had to show them that I could catch some of these trout. So
much for a so-called expert showing his class how to catch trout during a
Trico hatch. Now it was time to panic. I grabbed one of those weighted Tricos that I had made years before and tied it onto my tippet two feet behind a
Patriot dry fly in a tandem setup. My luck was about to change: In the next
hour I caught a half-dozen trout on that sunken spinner. By the end of the
spinner fall, some of the registrants came over to me and congratulated me.

Next time you see thousands of spinners floating on the surface
and can't catch a trout, tug on that imitation and purposely sink it under
the surface. You might be surprised by the success you experience fishing a sunken spinner.

Has fishing spinner falls frustrated you? Have you had meager success
when fishing spentwings? Then remember these simple rules: Make the
cast as drag free as possible, try fishing the spinner imitation from an up-

stream position, don't overlook those early-season spinner falls, match the color and size of the adult as closely as possible, and remember that sporadic duns can create concentrated spinner falls. Finally, don't forget if all else fails, tug that spentwing pattern underneath and fish it as a wet fly. Better yet, tie up some patterns that are designed to sink. Following these few simple rules can lessen some of the frustrations with spentwings.

TYING THE SPENTWINGS

You'll see several patterns with a lot of innovations in this chapter. I've included a pattern that has a twisted body, a sinking Trico pattern, and others.

If you've tied or fished spentwings for any length of time, you've probably encountered some problems. First, since these flies are fished flush with the surface, they are difficult to follow. Russ Mowry of Latrobe, Pennsylvania, was possibly one of the finest and most innovative fly tiers I have known. Russ always had a short post on his spentwing patterns so they were easier to follow. Tie in a short piece of bright poly like Mike O'Brien does on his Coffin Fly pattern later in this chapter.

Other challenges of tying spentwing patterns include creating lifelike flies, splitting the tails, and placing the wings. With the advent of new materials (see Red Quill Spinner), creating a lifelike spentwing that floats has become simpler. Wing materials such as organza and a myriad of synthetics help you get that lifelike appearance. Placing these wings on the hook properly can be a nasty problem. Make certain you dub a bit of poly on the tying thread and make a few turns over and around the wing in a figure-eight fashion to secure them. This also builds up the thorax area. Don't overlook the two methods of tying in hackle for spentwings that I mention later in this chapter while tying the Green Drake and Coffin Fly. They both create lifelike spinner wings.

Creating a lifelike pattern can be a problem, especially with some of the intricate body shadings on the natural. The twisted bodies of the Green Drake Spinner and the Coffin Fly are similar to the Brown Drake tied in Chapter 8. If you look closely you'll see that some of the larger natural duns and spinners have distinct markings on the sides of their abdomens. By adding a piece of thread or a few strands of yarn and twisting that thread or yarn with a small piece of poly, you get the desired markings on the sides of the body.

I did an experiment on the stream recently with two Trico spentwing patterns. I fished for a half-hour with one pattern that had the three tails clumped together and caught one trout. I then switched to a second pattern where the tails were neatly divided. That second pattern caught three trout. That split tail on the second pattern was the only difference between the two. Was it the split tail? Try separating the tails on your spentwings. Follow the directions given in the section on the Red Quill Spinner.

SOME IMPORTANT MAY AND JUNE SPINNERS—THE SULPHUR, GRAY DRAKE, AND DARK BROWN SPINNERS

Late May and early June is my favorite time of the entire fishing season. In *The Hatches Made Simple,* I show in a couple of tables when most of the hatches appear and at what time of the year they appear. The majority of hatches in the East and Midwest appear in late May and early June. The peak of hatching activity in the West occurs a month later. It is at this time that you'll finds sulphurs and pale morning duns making their annual appearances. Also at that time you'll see spinners of the gray drake and more dark brown spinners. All three—plus more—can produce some fantastic spinner falls. The gray drake is one of the top spinner falls in the Midwest. Although the dun seldom produces many rises, anglers look forward to the evening spinner fall.

If you have difficulty following the drift of spentwing artificials, follow the suggestion for the Sulphur tied below. I said earlier that Russ Mowry, a well-known fly tier from western Pennsylvania, tied all of his spentwing patterns with a small upright post similar to that of a parachute fly. This small post makes the pattern much easier to see. Try adding posts to some of your favorite patterns.

Dressing: Dark Brown Spinner (*Paraleptophlebia*)
Hook: Mustad 94833, Size 18.
Thread: Dark brown.
Tail: Dark brown hackle fibers.
Body: Dark brown poly.
Wing: White poly yarn, tied spent.

Dressing: Gray Drake Spinner (*Siphlonurus*)
Hook: Mustad 94831, Size 12.
Thread: Gray.
Tail: Moose mane fibers.
Body: Medium gray poly.
Wing: Dun hackle; follow tying procedure for Twisted Spinner.

Dressing: Sulphur Spinner or Pale Morning Spinner (*Ephemerella rotunda, inermis,* and *dorothea*)
Hook: Mustad 94840, Sizes 16, 18, and 20 (for *E. dorothea*).
Thread: Tan.
Tail: Tan deer body hair.
Body: Tan poly (very pale cream for *E. dorothea*).
Wing: Pale gray poly yarn, tied spent or upright.

1. (Sulphur) Tie in tan thread and wind back to the bend. Tie in a half-dozen tan deer-hair fibers for the tail.
2. Tie in the wing before you wind the poly forward. Use a good amount of poly. Let the poly wing stand upright as a post for now.
3. Dub tan poly and form the body. Wind up to the wing.
4. *Split the poly wing into thirds. One third becomes the right wing, one third the left wing, and one third an upright wing. Pull the right and left spent wings and tie them in so they lie flat. Make some wraps around the wing as*

Tricos in the air mean the Sunken Trico will be effective.

you would with a post in a parachute. Leave the third on top and clip it later so it's only a small stub.

5. *Take a red, orange, or yellow permanent marking pen and mark the small upright middle wing, or you can leave it as is. Clip off so it's only one-quarter inch high.*

6. Whip-finish.

THE SUNKEN TRICO

I just discussed the problem I encountered on the Ruby River trying to catch trout during a Trico spinner fall. I mentioned that I finally tried a weighted Trico Spinner. The spinner pattern had wings made of cream hackle, a body of black and cream angora, and a pale dun tail. Before I began tying the materials on the Size 20 short-shank hook, I added five turns of .005-inch lead wire to the body. I connected the pattern to the bend of the hook of a Size 16 Patriot dry fly. The dry fly acted as a strike indicator. When the Patriot sank I set the hook. I tied the Trico imitation about a foot and a half behind the dry fly and cast the two flies. That really saved the day for me.

Does that same pattern work on other waters? Bob Budd tried it on a heavily fished section of Spring Creek in central Pennsylvania during a Trico spinner fall. He caught a half-dozen trout on that pattern when the normal number of fish caught on the floating spinner during the fall might have been two or three. Tie up a few and try them.

Dressing: Weighted Female Trico Spinner
Hook: Wet-fly hook, Size 20 to 26.
Thread: Dark reddish-brown 6/0.
Tail: Rusty dun hackle fibers.
Body: White and dark brown opossum or angora dubbing.
Wing: Six strands of Flashabou.

1. *Take .005-inch lead and make five wraps around the shank of the hook.*
2. Tie in the dark brown thread and wind back to the bend of the hook. Tie in a few dun hackle fibers as a tail at the bend of the hook.
3. Make a turn or two of white angora or opossum dubbing over top of the tail. Tie in a couple of hackle fibers onto the left and right of the tail. Tie these side fibers in just in front of the dubbing. **Doing it this way makes the outer tails flare to the right and left.**
4. Dub in dark brown angora or opossum and wind up the shank to where you plan to place the wing.
5. Tie in the Flashabou wing. Dub some of the dark brown opossum over top of the wings in a figure-eight.
6. Shape the wings by cutting both sides. Each wing should not be quite as long as the shank of the hook.

7. Finish off the head with some of the dubbed dark brown opossum, and then whip-finish and lacquer.

THE TWISTED GREEN DRAKE SPINNER—FLY FISHING FOR BROOK TROUT IN LABRADOR

There are two places that I've wanted to fly fish before I die—New Zealand and Labrador. New Zealand—I've been there and done that. I had my introduction to Labrador in July and August 2001. For several years I had heard great stories of the huge brook trout from Steve McDonald. Steve's an anesthesiologist from the Doylestown area of Pennsylvania. Give him a fly rod and he becomes Steve McDonald, avid fly fisher.

Steve and I traveled to Cooper's Minipi Camps just south of Goose Bay, Labrador, to find out just how good the brook trout fishing was. What a spectacular way to introduce me to fly fishing in Labrador. The float plane landed within a hundred feet of the lodge on Anne Marie Lake. For the next week Steve, seven other anglers, and I would call Anne Marie Lodge home.

The first night we arrived the giant green drake hatch of the north (*Hexagenia rigida*) made its appearance. We could look forward to a week of matching hatches and spinner falls to rising four- to eight-pound brook trout. That first evening thousands—no millions—of huge yellow mayflies popped onto the surface. A Size 6 or 8 long-shank hook with a body of pale yellow and olive wings would match the hatch adequately. Ralph Coles, our guide for the evening, directed the canoe toward a section of the Minipi River system locals call Loverboy.

The Minipi River system is an unusual area. You'll see lakes and ponds with rivers flowing in and out of them. The faster sections might be only a few hundred feet long. Many of the bigger brook trout live in the lakes and some of the smaller fish in the faster sections. Northern pike coexist with the brook trout in these lakes and ponds.

That first evening we fished it seemed like every green drake in Canada decided to appear on the water. Millions and millions decided to appear on the surface that evening and the extremely cool late July evening prevented all but a few of the hardiest from taking flight. About 8:30 P.M. our guide drifted the canoe into a small cove. The area was lined with lily pads and three heavy risers sipped in a dun or two and then moved on. Minipi brook trout sip in a dun and then move to another location fifteen to thirty feet away from the first rise. I think they constantly move because of conditioning brought on by predators like the osprey and northern pike. Which way the trout would head for their next morsel was extremely difficult to predict. A trout finally boiled at Steve's pattern and he fought a four-and-three-quarter-pound Minipi-bred brook trout. Duns emerged and trout fed for more than two hours that first evening.

The evening proved to be a harbinger of things to come—great hatches and spinner falls and heavy rising trout for the next week. The same hatch and fall continued to appear for the entire week, and every evening we landed some heavy trout on dry flies. Steve McDonald caught one of the biggest fish of the week—an eight-pound brook trout that took a different version of a Yellow Stimulator called the Laid Back Hex (see Chapter 10). (John Clarke, one of the other anglers at the lodge, landed one eight-and-a-quarter pounds the very next evening.) That Stimulator type pattern worked especially well when we saw trout chasing emergers. The two of us caught ten trout over four-and-three-quarter pounds on that Stimulator type pattern. I'm convinced that the down wings suggest an emerging dun to the trout.

On several evenings at dusk, trout fed on spent green drake spinners. When they fed on these dead mayflies they didn't move as far for their next rise. Maybe it was because it was darker or the spinners were more concentrated, but their movements seemed to be much more predictable. Steve and I used Twisted Green Drake Spinners and Convertibles (see Chapter 10) on those evenings when the brookies rose to spent-winged naturals.

Dressing: Twisted Green Drake Spinner
Hook: Mustad 94831, Size 8 or 10.
Thread: Pale yellow.

Body: Creamish-yellow poly or yellow Flex Wrap twisted with brown
thread.

Wing: Two grizzly hackles trimmed on the top and bottom, or pull half
to the right and the other half to the left and tie in like posts on a
parachute.

1. Tie in the yellow tying thread and wrap the shank of the hook completely. End up with the thread at the bend of the hook.
2. *Tie in a piece of stiff pale yellow poly yarn or Flex Wrap near the bend of the hook. Tie in with the poly a piece of brown sewing thread or heavy tying thread. Take the poly and the brown thread and place into a hackle pliers. Spin the two about twenty times and bring the end attached to the hackle pliers to the other end attached to the shank.* **The poly and the thread should now curl up and form a great tapered body with brown markings.** *If they don't, try again. Make certain that the brown thread is tight.*
3. Tie in and make certain that the body extends back over the bend of the hook. Tie in the front of the twisted body just above the point of the hook. Dub additional pale yellow poly dubbing and complete the rest of the body up to the wing.
4. Tie in two extra-large grizzly rooster hackles. Make about ten turns with the hackle and tie off both.
5. *Take the right half of the hackle and wind around the base. Next take the left half of the hackle and wind around the base. Wind each as you would a post on a parachute pattern. Make certain you take half of the hackle on the top and bottom and tie this in with the side hackle.* **Using this technique negates cutting the top and bottom hackle.** *Alternate method: Cut off the hackle on the top and bottom.*
6. Tie off and whip-finish.

THE TWISTED COFFIN FLY SPINNER

Talk about innovative fly tiers—Mike O'Brien is one of the top. His patterns are some of the best I've seen in my fifty years in the sport. He has

Mike O'Brien ties his Twisted Coffin Fly Spinner.

tied flies for more than thirty years. Mike and Jerry Stercho publish the *Mid Atlantic Fly Fishing Guide* (Box 144, Allenwood, PA 17810-0144). That magazine has timely topics on hatches, patterns, streams, and tactics for the Northeast.

When Mike's not editing his magazine, he's guiding near his Williamsport, Pennsylvania, home on the Susquehanna River. He guides more than sixty days a year. Of those, about fifty are fly-fishing trips for carp—yes, I said for carp. He has made a science of catching these bottom feeders on patterns like the O'Brien's Crayfish Clouser.

One of Mike's favorite techniques is twisting the body. He first began tying these twisted patterns back in the late seven-

The coffin fly spinner natural.

ties. I recently had an opportunity to sit down and watch Mike tie a Twisted Coffin Fly Spinner. He uses the same tying procedure to tie many of his cricket, hopper, inchworm, caddis, and large spent-winged drake patterns. Mike uses several unusual techniques to finish his pattern. First he places the butts of two or three long moose mane fibers in the eye of a large needle. He inserts the needle in the tip of the twisted abdomen and brings the needle out at the front end of the twisted body.

Mike also has other useful techniques when he ties this pattern. He doesn't cut off the end of the poly yarn. After he finishes the twisted part of the body, he dubs and winds white poly on the front half of the body. That dubbed white poly is wound over the poly yarn. He uses the excess poly yarn at the front as a short post. This post serves to wrap the hackle around, parachute style, and helps him follow the pattern easily on the water. When he ties off the tip of the hackle he pulls all the wound hackle fibers upward so he doesn't crimp them.

Tie the Twisted Coffin Fly for those fantastic spinners in the East in late May and June. If you plan to use this recipe for other drake spinner falls, tie some with tan, maroon, dark brown, and dark gray bodies.

Dressing: Twisted Coffin Fly Spinner

Hook: Mustad 94831, Size 8 or 10.

Thread: White.

Tail: Three long moose mane fibers.

Body: White poly yarn or Flex Wrap and white poly for dubbing.

Post: White poly yarn.

Spentwings: (Optional): White poly yarn.

Hackle: A grizzly hackle.

1. *Mike takes a piece of white poly yarn and holds one end in each hand. By rolling the poly yarn between his thumb and index finger, going in opposite directions in each hand, he twists the poly tight. After it is tight, he simply pushes his hands together and the poly will roll or curl, forming the twisted*

body. He places the tip of the twisted poly out over the bend of the hook. For this pattern Mike extends the body about an inch beyond the bend.

2. Tie in the white twisted poly where the body is over the point of the hook. Don't cut the poly yarn off—dub over this and use it as a post at the front.

3. *Take three long moose mane fibers and place the butts through the eye of a fairly large needle. Place the needle though the tip of the abdomen and bring out at the front of the twisted body.*

4. *Tie down the butts of the tail and wind the thread forward one-eighth of an inch behind the eye. Make about two dozen wraps with the tying thread around the poly post. Wind the thread high (**about a quarter of an inch to make the post sturdy enough to hold the hackle later**). Don't cut the post at this point; wait until the pattern is finished.*

5. *Dub white poly and complete the body. Begin the dubbing process where the twisted body ends and continue up to the post.*

6. *Tie in a fairly large grizzly hackle. Make about six to eight turns with the hackle around the white poly post. Let the hackle pliers hold the hackle on the shank after the last wrap. Let it lie over the hook while you tie it off. Pull all hackle upward and tie off the remaining hackle tip. Tie off and clip the tip.*

7. *Dub a small amount of white poly and wind it for the head.*

8. Whip-finish.

9. *Now cut off all but about a quarter inch of the post above the parachute hackle.*

THE RED QUILL SPINNER

Ah, those first days of trout fishing in April—how I look forward to them in anticipation of some great match-the-hatch events. In a period of just a couple weeks you can fish over trout rising to hatches like the little blue-winged olive dun, blue quill, quill Gordon, hendrickson, and black quill. If you've fished some of these well-known hatches that appear in April, you already know that these insects have a lot in common. First, most duns and spinners appear on the surface from noon to 5 P.M. Hatches will occur earlier and later, but the normal time is early afternoon. Second, if you look at these duns closely, you'll see that most are dark gray in color (especially on the back). That's why fly fishers find patterns like the Hendrickson, Blue Quill, Quill Gordon, and Adams extremely productive in April.

Third, the spinners of many of these mayflies are also similar in color. Female spinners appear on the stream to lay their eggs a day or two after the duns emerge. Spinners appearing this time of year usually have body colors that range from dark brown to dark reddish-brown. With two patterns, in Sizes 12 to 18, you will be able to match most April duns and spinners you'll encounter on waters across the country. My choice for the best pattern to match the returning egg-laying phase of many mayflies is the Red Quill Spinner.

When did I first use a Red Quill Spinner pattern? It was more than thirty years ago that I fished Pine Creek in north-central Pennsylvania one mid-April afternoon with the late Russ Mowry. Russ was not only one of the best and most creative fly tiers I knew, but he also freely shared his knowledge of fly fishing with everyone.

Russ and I hit a section of Pine Creek that day just a few miles downstream from Slate Run. Shortly after we arrived a good number of female red quill spinners mated and fell onto the surface, and dozens of trout rose to the spent spinners in the riffle in front of us. Both Russ and I tied on Red Quill Spinners and began picking up trout. That spinner fall lasted for almost an hour, and then the surface was again still and no trout rose. On what I had planned to be one of my final casts, my spinner pattern accidentally sank beneath the surface. It drifted a couple inches under the surface, a trout struck, and I set the hook. On the next couple of casts I purposely tugged the spinner pattern so it sank. Even though no trout rose, they fed underneath, and Russ and I continued to catch trout for the next half-hour.

Why did the sunken pattern work? Because the mayfly spinners that had landed on the surface upstream had sunk underneath the surface and the trout fed on them. I indicated earlier that the Red Quill Spinner copies many mayfly spinners found in April. One of these is the hendrickson spinner.

I have one difficulty fishing spent spinners: I have trouble follow-ing these low-profile flies on the surface. That's why I tie the pattern with light-colored wings. There are many wing materials you can use for spent wings. You can follow the procedure for tying in a low post of white poly used in the Coffin Fly Spinner. In the past decade dozens of materials have arrived on the market to copy the wings of spinners. I still prefer to use white, pale gray, or cream poly yarn or organza. This latter material floats well and is highly visible to the angler. Tie the pattern in Sizes 12 to 18.

Dressing: Red Quill Spinner

Hook: Fine dry-fly hook, Size 12 or 14.
Thread: Dark reddish-brown.
Tail: Rusty dun hackle fibers.
Body: Dark reddish-brown poly dubbing. (Optional: Rib the body with tan thread.)
Wing: White poly yarn or organza.

1. Tie in the dark brown thread and wind back to the bend of the hook.
2. Tie in a couple of hackle fibers for the tail in the middle of the shank.
3. *Make a turn of body dubbing over top of the tail. Tie in a couple of hackle fibers onto the left and right of the middle tail. Tie these side fibers in just in front of the dubbing.*
4. *Alternate method: Make a harness with a six-inch piece of the tying thread. Double the loose piece of tying thread and place the loop down and over the point of the hook. Bring the loop up to the tail. Now bring the two pieces of thread so they split the tail fibers in approximately three equal parts. Pull on the ends of the thread until you get the desired spread and tie in front of the tail.* **Using this technique gives you a great splayed tail and is much quicker than the first method.**

5. Dub and wind the poly body about three-quarters of the way up the hook. (On some patterns, you might want to tie in a piece of tan thread at the tail and rib the body.)
6. *Tie in the white poly wing or about ten strands of organza.* Wind some of the dubbed reddish-brown poly over the top of the wings in a figure-eight. **Wind over and around the wings to form a robust thorax.**
7. Shape the wing by cutting both sides to equal length. Each wing should be as long (or a bit shorter) than the hook shank.
8. Finish off the head with some of the dubbed poly. Whip-finish and lacquer.

You've just tied seven new patterns and used eleven new techniques. Keep tying the flies and using the techniques that you like.

7

Down-Wings

1. Adding a tail to a caddis pattern to create a more stable pattern (Black Caddis, step 2, Fluttering Deer-Head Caddis, step 4, and Deer-Head Caddis, step 3)
2. A different way of adding a hackle to a down-wing (Fluttering Deer-Head Caddis, step 6)
3. Adding two hackles to a down-wing pattern (Fluttering Deer-Head Caddis, steps 5 and 6)
4. A different type of wing style for down-wing patterns (Deer-Head Caddis, steps 2, 3, and 6)
5. Making the thorax of the down-wing a different color than the body (Deer-Head Caddis, step 4)
6. Forming a segmented caddis body from poly yarn or Flex Wrap (Twisted Caddis, steps 1 and 2)
7. Using a short-shank or smaller hook for a down-wing pattern (Twisted Caddis, step 1)

8. Using one hackle for the front of the body and the thorax (Twisted Caddis, steps 2 and 3)
9. Making a down-wing for a large stonefly or caddisfly (Simple Salmon, step 3)
10. How to make a caddis wing out of trimmed deer hair (Kurt's Caddis, step 4)
11. How to reinforce peacock bodies with the tying thread (Kurt's Caddis, step 2)

Down-wings are important and an essential part of every angler's fly box. I carry hundreds of these patterns on every fishing trip. Why are they called down-wings? A mayfly dun usually has wings upright when at rest. They are copied by parachute or upright-winged patterns. A mayfly spinner usually has wings spread outward in a spent position after it has laid its eggs and when it lies flat on the surface. Fly fishers often copy spinners with spentwing imitations. Caddis and stoneflies have wings that lie down just above the body when at rest (caddisflies often have wings in a spent-like form after egg laying). On down-wing patterns that copy caddisflies and stoneflies the wings extend back over the body and out over the bend of the hook.

FISHING THE DOWN-WINGS

There are hundreds of different caddis emerging across the United States and Canada. How can you have enough patterns to match all of these hatches? Caddis and stoneflies come in a limited number of body colors, so you can make a good selection of sizes and body colors and feel confident that you'll match the vast majority of down-wings appearing. I first mentioned in *How to Catch More Trout* that I usually use a couple of Wheatley fly boxes that include, in different compartments, bodies of cream, tan, brown, green, gray, and black. For each of these colors I have patterns tied in Sizes 12 to 20. You'll match the vast majority of down-wings with these body colors and sizes (Table 3.)

Table 3. The patterns and sizes that match most caddisfly hatches

SIZE	COLOR OF BODY	COLOR OF BODY	COLOR OF BODY	COLOR OF BODY	COLOR OF BODY	COLOR OF BODY
12	Cream	Tan	Brown	Green	Gray	Black
14	Cream	Tan	Brown	Green	Gray	Black
16	Cream	Tan	Brown	Green	Gray	Black
18	Cream	Tan	Brown	Green	Gray	Black
20	Cream	Tan	Brown	Green	Gray	Black

I had a deadline. I had to finish an 80,000-word manuscript on *Meeting and Fishing the Hatches* within a couple of months. I had never fished Western waters before and I planned to fish twenty rivers in three weeks. Fishing on that extended initial Western trip suddenly became a job rather than enjoyment. I didn't have time to really savor the rivers I fished. I fished much of the day, then went back to the motel and wrote about the day's experience. If I needed any special patterns for the next day of fishing I tied them that evening. I went to bed around midnight and got up the next morning around 7 A.M. to fish another river. What a grind! I had just finished fishing the Bitterroot River for two days and then Rock Creek for one day, and now I was heading upriver on the Clarks Fork to the town of Anaconda, Montana. People have been cruel to the river in this area. They had polluted the heck out of it and it was still in a recovery stage when I fished it.

I asked a landowner if it was okay to fish and then headed to the forty-foot-wide river. Not one mayfly emerged that evening and I was about ready to quit. One more cast—you know the procedure—then I'd head back to the car. In the few seconds that cast and drift took to complete, I saw a few moth-like insects just above the surface and moving upriver. Trout came completely out of the water for these fairly large caddisflies. Within minutes that riffle in front of me came alive with a dozen brown trout chasing emerging caddis. I carried an insect net with me so I could collect insects I'd later identify. I captured one of the caddisflies, noted its dark brown body, and tied on a Size 14 pattern to copy it. I didn't have to wait long to see if the down-wing pattern worked. Did you ever experience a day of fishing where you caught a trout on the first or second cast and never caught another one? That didn't happen that evening. A heavy brown trout took the fly on almost every cast in that riffle. I ended the evening an hour later, weary from the day of fishing but happy for the success I had experienced. The pattern I used that evening had a body of twisted material. I have since used poly yarn to make the body with the same technique.

The next day I headed for the Kootenai River in northwestern Montana. I met up with an old fishing buddy, Al Gretz, that evening, and we fished several miles downriver from Libby, Montana. That evening on the Kootenai River, a tan caddis appeared and rainbows fed for more than an hour. I used the same twisted caddisfly with a tan body, and it too caught plenty of trout.

TYING THE DOWN-WINGS

If you've fished down-wing patterns, then you already know that there are several inherent problems with them. First, because of their low profile, they are often difficult to follow on the surface. To overcome this you can raise the profile, add a brighter color to the down-wing, or fish the pattern behind another brighter, easier-to-see dry fly. It's a tradeoff. Caddis patterns should be fished with a low profile to copy the naturals, but if you want to follow the fly then use a hackle in the front as in the Fluttering Caddis or one palmered on the body as in the Henryville pattern. If you opt for the lower-profile pattern, then add a bright piece of poly yarn on top of the down-wing or use a tandem with another, brighter pattern.

A second problem with the down-wing pattern is its lack of buoyancy. You can alleviate this by using the Twisted Caddis pattern and extending the body out over the bend of the hook. If you're tying a Size 14 caddis pattern, then use a Size 16 hook or a short-shank Size 14 and twist the poly yarn for the body and extend it beyond the bend. The body in reality becomes the tail and adds balance to the fly. A word of caution when you tie this pattern: Don't make the twisted body extend too far beyond the hook. If the "tail" section is too long, it will get caught under the gap of the hook. Another way to solve the buoyancy problem is to add a shuck to the pattern. This shuck becomes a tail and is extremely effective when caddis are emerging.

If you've tied these patterns then you know there are at least two other problems with down-wings. First, the hackle is difficult to wrap around the hair wing head, and even once it is wrapped it tends to loosen after catching one or two trout. Second, the wing is often difficult to anchor properly. Wing placement on many of the down-wings looks awkward at best. Hackle in the Fluttering Caddis can slide off the small head. The area where you wind the hackle is also narrow and this tends to cramp the hackle. Additionally, the hackle tends to come loose quickly. You can overcome both hackle problems by following the tying procedure for the Fluttering Caddis (step 6 for a different way of anchoring the hackle) and Deer-Head Caddis.

You'll find several unusual tying techniques in this chapter to help you overcome some of the problems with down-wings. A head is formed for the Deer-Head Caddis by tying in the deer hair and extending the tips out over the eye of the hook. After you've dubbed the thorax, bring the deer-hair tips back over the hook and tie them in. This forms a perfect head and allows you to add a different color for the thorax.

You'll find another unusual technique when tying the Fluttering Caddis. Here the hackle is tied directly to the shank and not on the butt of the wing. The hackle is cut off on the top, or shoved to the right and left, before the wing is placed over it. By tying the pattern this way I get a much more lifelike caddis.

We'll look at the Black Caddis, Deer-Head Caddis, Twisted Caddis, Fluttering Caddis, and others and tie each. Remember to tie any of the patterns you prefer in several body colors and sizes.

THE BLACK CADDIS

Black-bodied caddisflies appear almost everywhere there's a trout stream. I've fished over great hatches on the Yakima in Washington, the Bitterroot in Montana, and Penns Creek in Pennsylvania. Whether they're called the Mother's Day hatch in the West or the grannom in the East, they produce great fishing opportunities.

I'll never forget that Mother's Day caddis hatch on Washington's Yakima River. If you've ever experienced the gigantic grannom on Penns Creek or the Delaware River, then you already know you're in for some exciting match-the-hatch opportunities with caddis early in the season. But there's another caddisfly, albeit a bit smaller, that appears a few days earlier, and it too can create some great early-season fly fishing. Anglers call it the little black caddis.

I already talked about the Mother's Day caddisfly hatch in Washington. This down-wing appears near the middle of May and produces some great opportunities to match the hatch early in the season. That first day I met the hatch on the Bitterroot River, the Black Caddis with a Z-lon shuck proved an excellent selection.

Are you prepared to meet the black caddis hatch? If you plan to be on any of your favorite trout streams in late April or early May, make certain you have plenty of these patterns tied in Sizes 12 and 16.

Black Caddis (Grannom)
Hook: Dry-fly hook, Size 12 to 18.
Thread: Black.
Tail: None. (Optional: Add a piece of tan Z-lon.)
Body: Brownish-black poly for dubbing.
Wing: Dark brown deer hair.
Hackle: Dark brown hackle.

1. Wind in the black tying thread one-third of the way back from the hook eye.
2. *Optional: Tie in a tan piece of Z-lon at the bend of the hook.* **This Z-lon serves two purposes. First, it acts as a tail and stabilizes the fly on the surface. Second, it imitates a caddis emerging from its pupal case.**
3. Dub in black to brownish-black poly and wind forward almost to the eye of the hook. Leave room for the wings.
4. Take about fifteen dark deer-hair fibers and tie in just behind the hook eye. Don't crowd the eye. Have the tips extend back to a point

just beyond the bend of the hook. Make several tight turns with the tying thread to secure the butt section of the deer hair. Shape the butts to make a small head.

5. Tie in a dark brown hackle just behind the eye of the hook and wind it five to seven times around the shank just in front of the wings. Tie off. Note: The hackle on a Size 12 pattern should be one that is normally used for a Size 16 upright dry-fly pattern.

6. Whip-finish.

THE DEER-HEAD CADDIS

What an evening! Jim Misuira and the late Peter Kunis had invited me to fish with them on the Lackawanna River near Scranton, Pennsylvania. In the past two decades this great river has made a valiant attempt to return to its once prominent position as a top Pennsylvania trout stream. It has certainly succeeded. Some acid mine drainage still spills into the river, but it holds some hatches and plenty of heavy, stream-bred brown trout.

As we approached the river, a few March browns emerged but no trout showed. I decided to start with one of my favorite patterns—a down-wing called the Deer-Head Caddis. I tied on one of these patterns with the wings swept back over the tan poly–dubbed body. That pattern did not let me down that evening: I landed a half-dozen heavy browns on that down-wing before the three of us decided to quit.

That same deer-head pattern has proven successful across the United States and Canada. This caddis pattern with a black body caught a heavy brown on the Missouri River near Craig, Montana, and a nineteen-inch rainbow on the McKenzie near Eugene, Oregon. On central Pennsylvania's Little Juniata River, a green-bodied Deer-Head Caddis caught a nineteen-inch brown trout in early May. That caddis imitation also caught a five-pound brook trout on Labrador's Minipi River in the middle of the day. I've used the Deer-Head Caddis for more than fifteen years, and it has been one of my favorite patterns when I want to copy many of the down-wing hatches.

I said earlier that down-wing patterns copy stoneflies and caddis-flies. Both types of insects, when at rest, have their wings folded back over their body. What's different about the Deer-Head Caddis from other caddis patterns? Most caddis patterns are tied in with the butt section of the deer hair facing forward (toward the hook eye). These butts are then tied in just behind the eye of the hook. With the Deer-Head Caddis you use deer hair, but make it longer than normal and have the butt section tied in facing the rear (the tips of the deer hair extend out over the eye). These tips are then folded back over the body and tied in just behind the eye (similar to the Fulsher Minnow).

What are the advantages of the Deer-Head Caddis over other caddis patterns? The Deer-Head Caddis seems to float better, has a distinct caddis-like head, and allows the tier to make a thorax of a different color. If you examine a natural caddis, you'll see that some have a thorax with a slightly different color than the body. Tying a Deer-Head Caddis allows you to attain that variation in color.

Tie up a series of Deer-Head Caddis patterns in Sizes 12 to 16 with bodies of black, dark brown, tan, cream, and green. That way you'll be prepared for many of the caddisfly hatches you'll see.

I add a hackle to most caddis patterns to make them float better. On some of the patterns I cut the hackle off the top and the bottom so the pattern rests more flush with the water.

You'll encounter one difficulty when tying this pattern: judging the length of the wing. Normally what I do when tying the conventional caddis pattern is make the wing extend just a fraction of an inch back over the bend of the hook. With the Deer-Head Caddis you've got to estimate how far the wing will extend backward. What you do is tie in the wing just behind the eye, and then dub some of the poly dubbing at the thorax. Make certain the tying thread is back from the eye a quarter-inch (on a Size 12 hook). Then bring the wing up and over the dubbed thorax and tie it in. Practice several times if you're not pleased with the length of the wing. On a regular Size 12 hook I usually make the wing about a half-inch long. After tying a few patterns you'll find it relatively easy to estimate the length of the wing.

In the tying example below I use tan poly dubbing for the body, but remember you can tie this pattern with any color body material you want. Add the hackle where the head of the caddis ends and the wing begins. If you're tying a Size 12, use hackle that you'd normally use for a Size 16 dry fly.

The next time you encounter a caddis or stonefly hatch be prepared with a Deer-Head Caddis imitation. After you've used the pattern, you too will consider it one of your favorites.

Dressing: Deer-Head Caddis (Tan)
Hook: Dry-fly hook, Size 12 or 18.
Thread: Tan.
Tail (optional): Tan Z-lon.
Wing: Deer hair.
Body: Tan poly dubbing (if you prefer you can substitute green, brown, black, brown, or cream), ribbed with brown hackle.
Hackle: Dark brown.

1. Tie in the tan thread and wind back one-third of the way on the shank of the hook. *Tie in about two dozen dark deer hairs. The tips should extend out over the eye of the hook and the butt section of these should extend backward. A Size 12 caddis pattern should ex-*  *tend out beyond the eye about half an inch. Adjust other sizes accordingly.* Tightly wind about a half-dozen turns of thread over the butts to secure.
2. Dub dark tan poly on the thorax area only. Now wind back to the bend of the hook.

3. Optional: Tie in a two-inch piece of light tan Z-lon at the bend of the hook. Make several turns with the tying thread to secure and clip off so the shuck extends back over the bend almost the length of the shank of the hook.

4. Now dub tan poly on the tying thread and wind up to the thorax.

5. *Pull the deer hair back over the body and tie in at the thorax. At first you might have difficulty judging the length of the wing.* **This method forms a perfectly rounded head.**
6. Tie in a dark brown hackle. Make certain the shiny side (the darker or top side of the feather) is facing back and the dull side facing forward. Use a hackle you'd normally use for a Size 16 or 18 pattern. Tie in the hackle and wrap it to where you've just formed the thorax and head.
7. Now wind the hackle six or seven times around the hook where the wing ends and the head begins.
8. Tie off the hackle and whip-finish.

THE FLUTTERING DEER-HEAD CADDIS

I look forward to fly fishing early on summer mornings on limestone streams. On those midsummer trips I often encounter green caddis hatches. Where do you need a Green Caddis pattern? Just about any good trout stream across the United States holds green caddis. Whether you fish the McKenzie River in Oregon or the Delaware River in the East, you'll encounter down-wings with green bodies. Many of these caddis are members of the free-swimming *Rhyacophila* genus.

This pattern is a different type of down-wing—here you add the hackle before the wing is completed. It makes a lot of sense. Here you'll tie the hackle directly to the body rather than on the flimsy wing butt.

When you've finished wrapping the hackle, you can either cut off the excess on top or move the hackle to the right or left to make room for the wing. You can use the same procedure when you tie the Deer-Head Caddis. Try it—it's a very effective down-wing.

Dressing: Fluttering Deer-Head Caddis
Hook: Dry-fly hook, Size 12 to 16.
Thread: Green olive.
Tail: None. (Optional: Add a piece of tan Z-lon.)
Body: Olive green poly dubbing, ribbed with a brown hackle.
Wing: Elk hair.
Hackle: Brown hackle.

1. Wind in the tying thread one-third of the way back from the hook eye.
2. *Take about fifteen to twenty deer hair fibers and tie them in by the butts. Use a hair stacker to get the butts even. The tips will extend out over the eye. Make certain the wings are long enough. Later you'll pull them back over the top of the body.*
3. *Wind the thread back to the bend of the hook.*
4. Dub in the olive green poly and wind forward almost to the eye and over the butt. (The wing is still in a prone position and facing forward.)

5. *Tie in a brown hackle where you will tie in the wing. If you're tying a Size 14, use the size you'd normally use for a Size 16 or 18 fly, and wind the hackle five to seven times around the shank. Tie off. Clip off the hackle on the top where the*

wing will go or move it to the right or left. **There should be no hackle on the top half of the pattern.**

6. *Position the tying thread so it's about one-third of the way back on the shank. Now grab the deer hair and pull it over top of the body and tie in. Tie in a second brown hackle (normally what you'd use for a Size 16 pattern) where you've wrapped the head and made a few turns with the hackle.* **You now should have hackle (for a Size 18 fly) on the bottom of the body and another hackle (a Size 16 of a normal fly pattern) tied in and wound in the thorax area.**

7. Whip-finish and coat the deer-hair head with cement to prevent it from breaking.

THE TWISTED CADDIS

What a spectacular river! As we drifted through many sections of this one- to two-hundred-foot-wide river, with impressive rapids throughout, I glanced toward the high mountains. For a few minutes I honestly thought that I was fishing in Montana or Colorado. But this was the Lehigh River located in the heavily industrialized Northeast. This was the Lehigh River, just fifty miles from Philadelphia and seventy miles from New York City. This was the Lehigh River that had just emerged from years of abuse and pollution. The Lehigh had had almost insurmountable difficulties. It had sewage problems, nearly continuous chemical spills, and serious silting problems from some of its tributaries that flowed through anthracite coal fields. The section most affected by pollution was that part of the river from the town of Jim Thorpe downriver to Northampton—thirty miles of potentially prime trout water. The Lehigh River in the Pocono Mountains had been a great fishery for years, but the lower half of the river received heavy pollution. Fifty years ago the Lehigh River was a total mess—no fish and no hatches. If anyone had predicted to me then that many of these rivers would return and have some great trout fishing and spectacular hatches, I would have had them committed.

But guess what? Many of these local rivers have returned, and the Lehigh is at the head of the group. Fifty, even forty years ago, this section of the Lehigh River held no trout. Now it boasts a fantastic number of planted and stream-bred fish. This is the same Lehigh River where you can find a myriad of mayfly, stonefly, and caddisfly hatches through much of the fishing season. Down-wing patterns are especially important throughout the summer.

Are anglers finding out about the Lehigh River? You bet they are. Joe DeMarkis's guide service alone has floated the river for an average of 130 clients from April to June.

So this was a first for me—a McKenzie boat on the once heavily polluted Lehigh River. And to boot, the two boats were filled with fly-fishing gear. Forty years ago any local seeing us drift down the river would have laughed, but not anymore. As we began our float, I kept looking at the clear, clean, relatively cool water on that 94-degree afternoon. As we entered the river at noon, we recorded a 67-degree Fahrenheit water temperature. The two guides for the float trip were Chris Gatley and Dave Frey. Dave was the first guide on these waters; has floated the river for more than five years, Chris for a couple of years.

Dave guided Jim Slinsky and Irv Conway. Jim has his own syndicated radio show on the outdoors, and he and Irv are board members of the Lehigh River Stocking Association. Brian Tartar accompanied Chris and me for the first half of the trip. Brian is possibly one of the best fly fishers I have ever seen. He has an uncanny knack of spotting trout in the water. I don't care if they're six inches or three feet under the surface, Brian can spot them. Moreover, he can often entice them to come up for one of the caddis or terrestrial patterns that he often uses.

The hot late-June sun took its toll—the four of us caught fifteen trout before we took a late lunch break at 3 P.M. Fishing did pick up in the evening as a few tan caddis came back to the surface to lay their eggs for the next generation of down-wings. That's when I tested the Twisted Caddis and caught a couple of Lehigh River browns on the down-wing pattern.

The Twisted Caddis is extremely easy to tie and it's very effective. Tie some with tan, cream, olive, and dark brown bodies. Try tying the pattern on a smaller hook. Tie a Size 14 pattern on a Size 16 or 18 hook. You can do that with the extended body. The wing goes out over the bend of these smaller hooks, acts as a tail, and gives a lot of stability to the down-wing.

Dressing: Twisted Caddis
Hook: Dry-fly hook, Size 12 to 16.
Thread: Dark brown.
Body: Brown poly yarn.
Wing: Medium elk hair.
Hackle: Brown hackle.

1. Note: You can use a smaller hook and extend the body by using this method. Use a short-shank dry-fly hook. *Take a three-inch piece of dark brown poly yarn and tie in just in front of the bend of the hook. Tie in a three-inch piece of dark brown thread. Place hackle pliers on the loose end and flick it so the yarn is twisted about twenty times, or you can twist the material with your hands. Now bring the end with the hackle pliers toward the end tied in on the shank. The poly will curl and form*

a distinct shaped body. Place the tip out over the body to get the length you desire. Tie in the loose front end just above the point of the hook. The body should extend out over the bend of the hook. **Note: Don't extend the body out too far or it will catch in the gap of the hook.**

2. *Dub in brown poly dubbing and finish the body up to where you'll place the wing.*

3. *Tie in a hackle, make a few turns, and tie off. Either shove the hackle fibers on top to the right and left or clip them.*

4. Now tie in the elk hair out over the extended body. The wing should be slightly longer than the body. Make a half-dozen turns over the butt section. *The wing extended out over the extended body acts like a tail and gives buoyancy and stability to the pattern.*

5. *Continue winding the hackle over the butt section of the wing.*

6. Half-hitch, whip-finish, and cement.

THE SIMPLE SALMON

Nick Nicholas of West Yellowstone, Montana, first showed me this pattern. I'm not sure who developed this fly, but it evolved in the West. Nick guides on the Madison, and frequently he and his clients fish the famous salmon fly hatch on one of the nearby rivers.

Nick guided my brother, Jerry, and me several years back on the Firehole River in late June. This river holds a decent hatch of the giant salmon flies. When we arrived at the river a few of these large downwings returned to lay their eggs. When Nick saw a couple of trout chase the natural down-wings, he handed Jerry and me one of his Simple Salmon patterns. The pattern is a simple one to tie and very effective. It looks like about four down-wings tied on one long shank hook and it floats like a cork. Use this same technique for other down-wings and large wet flies.

Dressing: Simple Salmon
Hook: Mustad 94831, Size 6.
Thread: Orange.
Body: Dark orange poly dubbing.
Wing: Elk hair.

1. Wind the tying thread to the bend of the hook. Tie in a bunch of elk hair about the size of a matchstick back over the bend. Use a hair stacker to even the tips. Make this wing fairly short. Have it extend back over the bend about a quarter of an inch. It will be about one-third the length of a normal wing.

2. Tie in and dub orange poly dubbing just in front of the wing. Wind the dubbed poly up the shank of the hook about a half-inch.

3. *Tie in another wing of elk hair. Make this wing a bit longer than the first wing you tied in. Dub some more orange poly and wind that in front of the wing up the shank about a half-inch. Tie in a second wing and continue up to the eye of the hook until you've tied in at least four sets of wings. The final wing will be quite a bit longer than the first.* **This method makes the down-wing extremely buoyant and gives you a full wing.**

4. Shape the head, whip-finish, and lacquer.

KURT'S CADDIS

Do you want to use a down-wing that's easy to tie, floats like a bobber, and is extremely effective? Then you've got to try Kurt's Caddis. It has a lifelike silhouette and takes only a couple minutes to tie. With its body of clipped deer hair it will float all day.

The pattern resembles the Goddard Caddis but is much easier to tie. Kurt Thomas of Ridgway, Pennsylvania, first developed this pattern a couple of years ago. He uses the pattern extensively on some of his favorite small streams. The pattern not only copies many of the caddis but also can substitute adequately for a beetle or ant on those small streams you love to fish. But unlike other terrestrial patterns tied with deer hair, Kurt's Caddis is much more durable.

This pattern calls for a peacock underbody. You can substitute any other buoyant material such as brown, black, cream, olive, or tan ostrich.

Dressing: Kurt's Caddis
Thread: Dark brown.
Hook: Mustad 94840, Size 14.
Underbelly: Peacock.
Body (top): Clipped dark gray deer hair.
Hackle: Dark brown.

1. Tie in thread at the front and wind it back to the rear and then to the front again. Cover the shank with the thread.

2. Tie in a single peacock herl at the front and wind to the rear. *Take the tying thread at the front and wind to the back with four or five turns over the peacock.* **This reinforces the peacock.**

3. *Take a bunch of dark gray deer the size of a matchstick and tie in on top at the bend. Have the tips of the deer hair extend backward out over the bend. Tie in near the butts of the deer hair. Pinch the deer hair tightly and make several tight wraps. Then make several more wraps with the tying thread over some of the butts to splay them.*

4. Clip the tips off the deer hair at an angle and make them about a quarter of an inch long. Don't let go of the deer hair—you'll now tie it in a second time.

5. Tie in that second bunch of deer hair. Follow the same procedure and tie off.

6. Even the deer hair by cutting off any stray hair on the sides or bottom. Even up all the clipped deer hair on the top.

7. Tie in a dark brown hackle in front. Make six turns.

8. Tie off and cement.

You've tied six down-wing patterns using eleven new techniques. I think the Deer-Head Caddis, Kurt's Caddis, and the Fluttering Caddis are especially important because they show you different ways to wrap hackle and form wings.

8

Parachutes

9. A second method of working with flexible posts (Little Blue-Winged Olive Dun, step 2)
10. How to adjust the post (wing) backward (Blue Quill, step 2)
11. One method of tying an extended body (Twisted Brown Drake, step 3; also see Chapter 10, Convertible, step 2)
12. A second method of tying an extended body (Twisted Brown Drake, step 4)
13. How to wind two hackles on a parachute pattern (Twisted Brown Drake, step 8)
14. Making the body two colors from twisted Flex Wrap (Twisted Brown Drake, step 4)
15. Making a loop to hold the hackle on a parachute tie (Slate Drake, step 9)

In the past decade I have relied more and more on parachute type dry flies. Parachutes have one wing, called a post, tied in upright. The hackle, usually only one, is then wrapped around the base of that post five to seven times. Only two things differ on a parachute pattern from a classical Catskill tie: the way the hackle is wound and the configuration of the wing. My whole outlook and thinking on what type of dry flies to use and how to fish them has changed considerably in the past few years. I personally feel a parachute dry fly is much more effective than the divided-wing, high-riding dry fly. Why? I feel the lower-riding profile of the parachute more accurately copies the natural mayfly. I also strongly feel that trout recognize this lower profile of the parachute pattern and strike it more readily.

FISHING THE PARACHUTES

I still remember the first time I used a Hendrickson parachute during a hatch. It happened on a cold, blustery day near the New York/Pennsylvania border on a small stream. By early afternoon, thousands of fairly large hendrickson naturals braved the cold weather and appeared on the

Virgil Bradford lands a rainbow trout on a Vernille-bodied Little Blue-Winged Olive Dun on Silver Creek in Arizona.

surface. They were, however, unable to escape the water's surface and rode for hundreds of yards in front of us. I tied on that Hendrickson parachute and it changed my thinking on dry flies forever. Six trout took dazed naturals in front of me, and all of them eagerly took my parachute. The action continued for more than two hours that afternoon.

The second occasion occurred a few weeks later. This time it was on the Arkansas River with Phil Camera and Don Puterbaugh. A hatch of pale morning duns appeared in late morning and I cast a conventional Catskill pattern to match the hatch. Most of the trout refused the pattern until Don cut the hackle off the bottom. I began catching trout with that lower-riding pattern until one trout tore the fly apart. I then switched to a parachute Pale Morning Dun and the action continued.

I am a firm believer in the value of parachute patterns. Try them and you'll agree.

TYING THE PARACHUTES

For many years I didn't use parachute type dry flies. I hated tying them. Tying a parachute had several troublesome flaws until I found tying methods to overcome these inadequacies. If you've tied these patterns then you've probably already encountered some of the same problems. One problem: If you use poly yarn or any other flexible material for the single upright wing, you'll find that it's almost impossible to wrap the hackle around that post. Why? As you wrap the hackle, the post gives way and the hackle unwinds. If you don't use the method I suggest below, then by all means use a strong post. Elk hair makes a terrific post for parachutes. Often a quick way to overcome the problem with a flexible post is to make a good number of turns around the post with the tying thread. On larger patterns, wrap the thread about one-quarter inch high. Making more wraps than necessary and higher will strengthen the post.

A second problem: Even after you've conquered wrapping the hackle around the post, the hackle has a tendency to slip up and over it. I can't count the number of times I had just released a trout from a parachute and the hackle slipped up and over the post.

There's a third flaw with this pattern: Some tiers find it difficult to tie off the hackle and add a whip-finish to the fly. When they complete the pattern they often crimp many of the hackle fibers. Mike O'Brien prevents this by pulling all the hackle up and then tying off (see the tying instructions for the Coffin Fly in Chapter 6).

If you encounter a problem with a flexible wing you can try the method I suggested above, and if that doesn't work try turning the fly upside down and attaching a weight to the post. I usually attach a hemostat to the post and then wind the hackle. If that doesn't work, try using a second vise and clamp in the wing material with that.

Some tiers overcome the second problem—hackle slipping up and over the post—by first winding the hackle high on the post and making succeeding turns lower. But if the hackle loosens for any reason the hackle will still slip off the post. I think there's a better solution first shown to me by Rick Whorwood of Hamilton, Ontario. Rick includes a three-inch piece of thread with the post and winds the hackle around that thread and the post. He then brings that piece of thread down over the hackle and ties it off just behind the eye. You'll learn this technique and much more when you tie the Slate Drake and Little Blue-Winged Olive Dun.

How can you alleviate the frustration of tying off a parachute pattern? Finish the fly upside down. Yes, upside down. A versatile rotary vise will allow you to complete the pattern by doing that. Turn the fly upside down so you won't tie off some of the hackle. You can also use the loop I suggest in step 9 when you tie the Slate Drake, or follow the directions for the Coffin Fly (Chapter 6) and pull the hackle up while tying off the hackle.

We'll tie four great parachute patterns in this chapter—the Slate Drake, the Vernille-bodied Little Blue-Winged Olive Dun, the Twisted Brown Drake, and the Blue Quill.

THE SLATE DRAKE

My son, Bryan, and I recently fished Little Pine Creek in north-central Pennsylvania on a cool overcast Memorial Day weekend. The temperature that day didn't rise above 55 degrees and a slight drizzle fell. We

A slate drake dun.

fished that day on the delayed-harvest section just upstream from Little Pine Creek Park. When we arrived streamside shortly after noon, we saw trout rising throughout a deep glide in front of us. I sat back and watched for a few minutes and captured two different mayflies emerging simultaneously—the blue-winged olive and the slate drake. For the first hour more trout seemed to key in on the blue-winged olive, but by late afternoon they began taking the slate drake dun. We tied on the Slate Drake pattern I discuss here and began catching trout. For more than an hour that pattern caught trout on Little Pine Creek. Finally, near 5 P.M., the hatch waned and trout stopped surface feeding, but they did freely take the parachute Slate Drake pattern.

Slate drakes emerge in an unusual manner. The nymph often swims to shore or to an exposed rock or debris, crawls out of the water, and then changes from a nymph to a dun. By crawling out of the water, slate drakes lessen the threat of being eaten by trout. Therefore, on many occasions, few of the duns are available to trout. But add an overcast day and high, fast water, and the duns tend to emerge on the surface. Slate drakes that emerge in fall tend to emerge in the water more than their spring counterparts.

Tie the pattern in Sizes 12 and 14. Use the larger pattern in spring for the first generation, and a Size 14 for the second hatch in fall. Why the difference in size? Because the natural emerging in fall has a shorter time to develop (from July to September) and it usually doesn't grow as large as the spring generation (which has from October to May to grow).

Dressing: Slate Drake
Hook: Mustad 94833, Size 12 or 14.
Thread: Dark gray.
Tail: Medium dun hackle fibers.
Body: Dark gray poly dubbing.
Post: Pale gray or white calf body hair or tan elk hair tied in a post.
Hackle: Dark brown or cree.

1. Tie in the dark gray thread and wind back one-third of the way on the shank of the hook. Tie in about a dozen to two dozen light gray calf body hair or tan elk body hair fibers. (An elk-hair post is much easier to wrap hackle around.) The tips should extend out over the eye of the hook. Remember, the upright post should be about as long as the shank of the hook. Wind about a dozen turns of thread in front of the elk hair to make it stand erect. Make a few turns with the tying thread around the base of the elk hair.
2. Tie in a few dun hackle fibers for the tail at the bend of the hook. Make several turns with the tying thread to secure them.
3. Dub the tying thread with dark gray poly and wind up to the post.
4. *Tie in a three-inch piece of gray tying thread and mix it with the gray calf-hair post (see alternate method in step 8).*
5. Tie in a dark brown or cree hackle. Make certain the shiny side (darker or top side of the feather) is up and the dull side faces down.

6. Now wind the hackle six or seven times around the base of the elk-hair post and the three-inch piece of tying thread. *Start winding the hackle by starting high on the post and working lower.* **This will prevent the hackle from slipping up and over the post.**

7. Tie off the hackle.

8. *Bring the piece of tying thread mixed in with the post down over the hackle and tie off at the eye of the hook.* **The tying thread, tied in this manner, prevents the hackle from slipping up and over the post.**

9. *Tie off the hackle in this manner: Make a fairly large loop with a 3X leader. Wrap the tying thread around the leader three or four times. Have the loop face out over the eye. The loose butts of the leader will face backward. Cut one of the leader butts so it's flush with the body. When you make your last turn with the hackle, place the hackle and pliers through the loop, or you can get a hemostat and place the jaws through the loop to grab the tip of the hackle. Once you have hold of the hackle tips and you're holding it through the loop, pull on the long butt piece until the hackle is neatly in place. Make several wraps to secure.*

10. *Turn the fly upside down and whip-finish, or pull all the hackle upward and out of the way.*

THE LITTLE BLUE-WINGED OLIVE DUN WITH A VERNILLE BODY

In an average year, fellow fly fishers give me dozens of flies that they've tied and ask me to try them. Many of these flies are unique—a different body material, an unusual wing, or a new tail. A good example: I told you already about a tier who gave me a Slate Drake pattern that included recycled recording tape (that stuff you see strewn along highways) for the body. I place most of these patterns in one of my seldom-used fly boxes. I place a very few that look good to me in my vest and try to test them. One of those given to me a few years ago was a Little Blue-Winged Olive Dun—with a twist. The fly had no tail and a body of fine olive Vernille (a type of fine chenille). It looked intriguing and lifelike, and I decided to test the pattern when the appropriate time occurred.

A year after I received that pattern, Brian Williams, Virgil Bradford, and I fished a small nondescript stream, Silver Creek in north-central Arizona, when a hatch of little blue-winged olives appeared. Just as we approached the bank, a stocking truck stopped and unloaded a couple hundred trout in the stream in front of us.

Snow squalls laid a light dusting near the stream. For April it was downright cold. As we fished we noticed that the trout that had just been stocked rose to some insects on the surface. Because of the cold weather these insects were unable to take flight. I grabbed one of the small mayflies, examined it, and determined that it was a little blue-winged olive. Just minutes after those trout were stocked they began feeding on the surface on these mayflies.

Both Brian and I tore off the Woolly Buggers we were using and tied on smaller dry flies to match the hatch. One problem—I had only one regular Little Blue-Winged Olive in my fly box. I tied the pattern on my tippet and handed Brian the Little Blue-Winged Olive with the Vernille body. The pattern was a parachute with a fine olive Vernille body and no tail. Brian tied on the pattern and began casting in the direction of more than a dozen rising trout.

First cast—Brian missed a trout. Second cast—he missed another trout. Third cast—he hooked a rainbow. Fourth cast—Brian caught another trout. On the first ten casts Brian had ten strikes—yes, ten for ten. We had only one problem that morning—we had only one of those darned patterns with us. In the meantime, while Brian had all that action, I caught only a couple of trout on my Little Blue-Winged Olive pattern. Almost every time I've seen Brian since that episode, he looks at me and says "Ten for ten" and shakes his head in disbelief.

The little blue-winged olive (*Baetis*) is extremely common across the United States and is found on many tailwaters. If you've fished great rivers like the San Juan in New Mexico or the Missouri in Montana, you already know how important this hatch can be.

This small mayfly is especially important in the Southwest. I'll never forget the day I took a walk in Mesa, Arizona, one weekday afternoon in January. I had just written an article about the little blue-winged olive and how common it is on Arizona streams. I was reviewing that article as I took my walk. As I walked in the middle of the city a little blue-winged olive landed right on my clipboard. That day I saw thousands of these mayflies in the middle of town.

Look for hatches on many of your favorite streams in the spring and fall. This small mayfly appears most often in the early afternoon and is especially important on cold, overcast days. I often call it the "lousy-day hatch" because it has a propensity to appear on those less-than-ideal, drizzly days. I've seen the hatch and trout rising to it every month of the year.

Since that first episode with the Vernille-bodied pattern, I have used that dry fly almost exclusively when I hit a hatch of little blue-winged olives. I've also used the

same tying method for the Sulphur and Blue Quill, and these patterns work well also. I tie Sulphur patterns in Sizes 16 and 18 with pale yellow-orange Vernille, and the Blue Quill in a Size 18 with dark gray Vernille. The smaller the pattern, the better the dry fly floats. Don't tie patterns any larger than Size 16—the Vernille tends to make larger patterns sink quickly. One other advantage with this pattern is that you can cut the body to match the size of the emerging natural.

I have difficulty following the drift of Little Blue-Winged Olives, Slate Drakes, Adamses, and other dark-colored patterns. That's why I use a white poly post on the Little Blue-Winged Olive. With its white post, even in a small pattern, the dry fly is much easier to follow.

I said earlier that tying a hackle around a flexible post like poly yarn presents some problems. The hackle doesn't want to go around the post but over it. I've developed a new procedure that works well. If you still have problems, tie in a post of light brown elk hair.

You'll note in the illustrations and in the Slate Drake article that when I tie parachute type patterns I include a piece of tying thread in the post. When I finish wrapping the hackle around the post, I bring that piece of thread down over the wound hackle and tie it off at the eye. That piece of thread, tied in that manner, prevents the hackle from climbing up over the post.

Try this method for tying some of your smaller flies. You'll find it easy to tie and a very effective pattern to use. Try this pattern the next time you hit a hatch of little blue-winged olives. You might be like Brian Williams and get ten for ten.

Dressing: Little Blue-Winged Olive Dun
Hook: Mustad 94833, Size 18 to 22.
Thread: Dark olive.
Body: Very fine olive Vernille.
Post: White poly yarn, white calf body hair, or light brown elk.
Hackle: Dark gray hackle.

1. Tie in the olive tying thread.
2. Take a small piece of white poly yarn, white calf body hair, or elk and tie in as the post. Make several turns in front of the post and then a few around the post at the base. *If you're using a white poly post, you can strengthen it by making additional wraps around the base of the post. Continue to wrap until the base is sturdy. Wind well up the post and make*

plenty of wraps with the tying thread. Wind the thread back to the bend of the hook. Completely cover the entire shank of the hook with the tying thread.

3. *Take a two-inch piece of fine olive Vernille and place it on top of the shank. Make about five turns of thread around the Vernille starting at the bend and working up to just behind the post.*

4. Tie a three-inch piece of tying thread in with the post. Tie in a dun hackle with the shiny side up just behind the post.

5. Turn the vise upside down so the post is now upside down. *Place a hemostat on the post and begin winding the hackle around the base of the post. Make about six or seven turns around the post with the hackle. Tie off the hackle and cut off the hackle tip.* **By placing the post upside down and holding it with a hemostat, it's much easier to wrap the hackle around the post. Otherwise, when the post is upright, the hackle is often impossible to wrap around the post.**

6. *Alternate method if you're using a flexible post: Place the white poly yarn in a second vise (the vise jaws of this second vise will be above the original vise). Make certain you use a second vise that is maneuverable so that once the poly is in the jaws it can be moved upward to tighten the post.*

7. Whip-finish. *Cut the rear end of the body and round it off with a match or lighter.* Careful: Don't get the match too close to the body or it will go up in flames.

THE SUMMER BLUE QUILLS

It first happened to me on a July fishing trip in eastern Idaho on the Henrys Fork. It occurred a second time—in late May—on the Little Colorado River a couple of years later. The Miracle Mile section of the North Platte in Wyoming also showed me the same event in August and September.

What occurred on those late spring, summer, and early fall mornings across the United States? I hit little-known but spectacular hatches of blue quills. Anglers normally look for this hatch in April on many streams, especially in the East and Midwest. That early-season hatch appears for more than two weeks. But many streams across the country hold several other closely related species—not as well known, but all members of the genus *Paraleptophlebia*. Some of the heaviest hatches of blue quills appear in the summer and continue well into October. But few anglers ever witness these midsummer hatches because many emerge rapidly from the surface and few trout rise to them.

One way to take advantage of this summer blue quill is to fish it when the weather is less than perfect. Look for the hatch on cool, overcast, drizzly mornings in June and July. I've hit these dreary days and great hatches across the United States. But there are other ways you can fish this hatch in good weather conditions.

Wherever you find the hatch, remember that these mayflies often escape rapidly from the surface, so you might want to use a dark brownish-black nymph pattern or an emerger. Trout most often take that phase of the mayfly, caddisfly, or stonefly that's easiest for them to capture. When a mayfly like the blue quill escapes rapidly from the surface, trout tend to take the nymph that is changing into a dun. Anglers call this stage the emerger (see Chapter 2). For that fleeting time when the mayfly transforms from an aquatic insect into an air-breathing one, it is extremely defenseless. Trout sense this and often take an emerger and neglect the dun. Fish the nymph or emerger on a tandem rig behind a Blue Quill dry fly and you'll find out quickly which phase of the insect the trout are taking.

What pattern best matches the hatch? Again, I prefer a Blue Quill tied parachute style. I use light gray or white poly as the post because it's much easier to detect on the surface, and I often add a shuck to the tail.

Have you ever examined tails on some of the dry flies you use? You'll see that a natural has two or three small tails. For years I've been convinced that dense tails on dry flies represent shucks more than they do tails to trout. So, for years we've been copying emerging duns and didn't know we were doing it.

More recently fly tiers have copied the natural with a Z-lon shuck attached at the hook bend. This adequately copies the dun trying to rid itself of the last vestiges of the nymphal stage. Use a shuck that copies the color of the nymph. On occasion I've added a piece of nylon stocking to the fly on the stream.

You'll see in step 4 that I suggest an easy way to use a dubbing loop. It's effective and easy. Try it and you'll probably never use another type of dubbing loop.

Dressing: Blue Quill

Hook: Dry-fly hook, Size 18 or 20.
Thread: Dark gray.
Tail: Medium to dark gray hackle fibers.
Body: Dark gray poly dubbing.
Post: Light gray poly yarn.
Hackle: Light to medium blue dun.
Shuck (optional): Dark brownish-black Z-lon.

1. Wind the dark gray tying thread back one-third of the way on the shank of the hook. Take a two-inch piece of light gray poly yarn a bit smaller than the size of a matchstick and tie it in as the post. Have the poly extending out over the hook eye. Lift the poly upright and make a half-dozen turns of thread in front to make the wing stand upright. *Make plenty of wraps with the thread around the post to make it more stable.*

2. *Take a piece of tying thread and tie in behind the post (or make a loop in the thread, tie off, and cut one end). Wrap this piece of thread around the post two or three times. Take the tying thread attached to the bobbin and wind it over the piece of tying thread three times. Now you can adjust the post backward if needed by pulling on the thread that you've tied in.*
3. *Tie in a half-inch piece of blackish-brown Z-lon at the bend of the hook.* **This will imitate the shuck.** Cut the shuck to the length of the shank.
4. *Make a three-inch loop in the tying thread and tie it off. Leave both ends attached at the shank. Place a generous amount of wax on this loop. Dub dark gray poly into the loop. Spin the bottom of the looped thread with a hackle pliers. Wind the dubbed material up to the post.*
5. Tie a two-inch piece of tying thread in with the post standing up (this is optional). Place a medium dun hackle with the shiny side up and tie in just behind the post. Wind the tying thread to the eye and wrap the hackle six or seven times around the base of the post.
6. *With the hackle tip still in the hackle pliers, lay the hackle tip on the shank of the hook. Now pull all the wound hackle upward and back and tie off the hackle.* Pull the piece of thread (step 5) at the post and bring it forward. Tie the thread off in front of the post. *Make a whip-finish with the wound hackle still held high.*
7. Apply cement.

THE TWISTED BROWN DRAKE

Over the past thirty-five years I can count on one hand the number of times I haven't had a good imitation to match a hatch. I quickly forget about most of the frustrating, poor matching-the-hatch events, but one of those failed attempts still haunts me even though it occurred more than a quarter-century ago.

I'll never forget that evening on Pine Creek at Cedar Run in north-central Pennsylvania. Jim Heltzel had just taken up fly fishing and we decided to fish one evening early in June. Around 7 P.M. we headed up the lower end of Cedar Run and hit the first couple of riffles on that excellent small stream. Around 8 P.M. we decided to head downstream and end the evening on Pine Creek. As we retraced our steps, we noticed some large mayfly spinners in the air. When we arrived back on Pine Creek we saw hundreds and then thousands of these same large, dark mayflies. I assumed they were March browns, so both of us tied on March Brown Spinners and began casting to dozens of feeding trout.

Trout fed everywhere, mostly on large, dark spinners returning to lay eggs and die. There were so many spinners in the air that you could hear the humming of their wings. Within reach of my cast I saw no less than a hundred trout eagerly taking this seemingly unending supply of food. What a terrific way to match the hatch. Jim and I began casting—and casting—with very little success. I finally switched to a Black Quill pattern and caught one trout. Can you believe it? One trout when I had more than a hundred feeding freely within casting distance.

When dusk arrived the spinner fall began to wane, but a few large duns of the same species appeared on the surface. Jim and I walked away from that event frustrated, confounded, disgusted, and shaken. I grabbed a couple of the large duns and spinners and looked at them carefully. I decided they were brown drakes, very close relatives of the green and yellow drakes. Guess what? I had no adequate copy to match the dun or spinner of that mayfly. In fact, until that day, I had not realized that this hatch appeared in any numbers in the Northeast. Yes, I had encountered a few of these brown drakes on the Beaverkill, but not enough to create a feeding frenzy. Since that confrontation with the brown drake on Big Pine Creek, I have not been without a good pattern to match the hatch and spinner fall.

The most important part of the natural to copy, and also the most difficult, is the yellowish-brown underbelly. I use poly yarn because it comes in dozens of shades. I spin the poly with a piece of brown tying thread. Spin the poly about twenty times with your hand to bring the two pieces together and it will double up on itself. When you bring the two ends together, part of the poly will curl. Use that part as the end of the body. If you add a piece of tying thread as part of the underbody, the body will have two colors—one yellow-brown and the other brown. In addition, the brown thread makes lines on the sides of the fly and effectively copies those on the brown drake, yellow drake, dark green drake, and many of the Hex hatches you'll encounter. I prefer to use pale elk to copy the wing of the dun.

There's a second material, called Flex Wrap, that you can use to tie the Twisted Brown Drake. While Flex Wrap is a bit more lifelike, it doesn't float as well as poly yarn. It's used to wrap under a bandage. Try getting some of this material in your local drugstore and dye it to the color you prefer. It takes only a couple of seconds to dye the material any color you need.

Have you ever been frustrated by your inability to match a hatch? Be prepared to match the brown drake hatch common in the United States and Canada and many of the other large hatches that have darker markings on the belly. Tie a few of these patterns and save them for those frustrating days in late May or early June. When this hatch appears it can be one of the most frustrating—or rewarding—of the entire season. We'll tie the pattern as a Brown Drake and a Green Drake.

Dressing: Twisted Brown Drake (or Green Drake)
Hook: Mustad 94831, Size 12 or 14.
Thread: Dark brown (yellow).
Tail: Moose mane.
Body: Yellowish-brown poly with a piece of brown thread (or Flex Wrap
   dyed yellow-brown with a smaller piece of brown Flex Wrap inside).
Post: Light brown elk tied as a post.
Hackle: One dark brown and one grizzly hackle.

Note: Materials for the Green Drake are in parentheses.

1. Wind dark brown thread back one-third of the way on the shank from the eye of the hook. Take about a matchstick-wide bunch of long, light brown elk-hair fibers. Use a stacker to even the tips. Tie the hair in by the butts with the tips extending out over the eye.

2. Make several turns in front to hold the hair in place. Because the body will be extended, the upright post should be a bit longer than the shank of the hook. Wind the tying thread back to the bend of the hook.

3. *Take a piece of fairly stiff yellowish-brown poly yarn or Flex Wrap. Make it the diameter of a matchstick. If you use Flex Wrap, use a piece about an inch wide and six inches long. Place one end of the poly and a piece of brown thread in a vise. Grab the other end of the poly and thread with a hackle pliers and spin both, or use your hands as described above. Take a bodkin and place it where you want the body to end. Now move the one end of the spun pieces toward the other end. They will double up along with the brown thread. If you spin with your hands, move the two ends together.*

4. *To obtain a two-color body, place a piece of dark brown Flex Wrap inside a yellow (or visa versa) piece and twist them.* **This produces a great two-color body.**

5. *Place the tip out over the hook and tie in the butt section of the poly just behind the post. A second way is to tie off the body on the shank opposite the hook point.*

6. *Take several moose mane fibers and place the butts in the eye of a large needle. Bring the needle through the center and front end of the twisted body and tie the moose mane off. (This won't work with the Flex Wrap.)*

7. Dub the remainder of the body up to the wing with poly dubbing the same color as the twisted part.

8. Tie in one brown and one grizzly hackle in back of the post. Both hackles should have the dull side facing downward. Tie in the brown hackle first. Make about five winds around the post and tie off. Now take the grizzly hackle and wind in the same manner. *Take your time with the second hackle and weave it over the first.* **By moving the hackle slowly up and down as you wind it over the first one, you're able to have more of the two hackles stand upright.** Tie off the second hackle.

9. Finish off the head and whip-finish.

If you have tied the patterns then you've tried fifteen new techniques. As I've said many times, use those you feel comfortable with and discard the others.

9

Streamers and Bucktails

TECHNIQUES YOU WILL LEARN IN THIS CHAPTER

1. How to position cheek feathers on a streamer perfectly (Lady Ghost, step 5)
2. How to position the wings on a streamer with epoxy (Lady Ghost, step 4)
3. One method of forming a shiny head on a streamer (Sparkle-Head Streamer, step 2 and 6)
4. How to place larger beads on the hook with ease (Golden Shiner, step 1)
5. How to place even more weight on a hook (Golden Shiner, step 2)
6. How to tease the belly of a fly to make it stand out (Golden Shiner, step 8)
7. Using epoxy to shape a lifelike head on a streamer (Golden Shiner, step 9)

8. Using epoxy (Golden Shiner, step 9) and clear fingernail polish (Bead-Head Woolly Bugger, step 7) to cover a bead or cone and to protect it from discoloring.
9. How to prevent material from slipping back over the bend by ribbing the body (Lady Ghost, step 1)
10. How to hold eyes in place with epoxy (Golden Shiner, step 9)
11. Another method of making a whip-finish with a pen for hooks with large eyes (Lady Ghost, step 6)

Streamers and bucktails can be an important part of a fly fisher's cache of patterns. Many of these imitate minnows, fish-fly larvae, and other life found in streams. One of my top-ten patterns for years has been the Bead-head Woolly Bugger. If you check many of our streams and rivers nationwide, you'll find many fish-fly larvae. The larva closely resembles a gray Woolly Bugger. That pattern has saved many a trip for me—and it still does to this day. The Lady Ghost is another one of those old standbys that seldom fails me. I've added some new synthetic to this standard pattern to make it even better. You'll learn to tie these and a couple other productive patterns and hopefully test a few new techniques.

FISHING STREAMERS AND BUCKTAILS

I often associate fishing streamers and bucktails with high, cold water—often early-season conditions—but they can be especially useful any time of the year in heavy water when you want to get deep fast. I link these large flies with fishing on or near the bottom. If you're not fishing them there, then you're not catching trout.

I mention later in this chapter a mid-May day on the Little Colorado River in northern Arizona where I learned the merits of the Bead-Head Woolly Bugger. No pattern—and I mean no pattern—worked that morning on Wink Crigler's stretch of the Little Colorado except the Woolly Bugger.

But some streamer type patterns produce all season long. Doug Matty is a major in the army. He has been an instructor at West Point for much of his career, and while there he was a member of the fly-fishing club. Doug uses a White Woolly Bugger type pattern all year long and does consistently well with it. I said "Woolly Bugger type" because it has all the amenities of a Woolly Bugger except it is white and there's no palmered hackle over the body. What's the secret to his success with this White Woolly Bugger? Doug believes in the White Woolly Bugger, uses it frequently, and consistently does well with it, even in midseason.

TYING STREAMERS AND BUCKTAILS

What are some of the inherent problems you run into when tying streamers and bucktails? Adding adequate weight to the pattern to get it deep quickly is one problem. There are other problems with streamers, most of which center around the tying of the fly. To get the pattern deeper faster, try the technique Chip Hidinger uses when tying the Golden Shiner. He doubles the lead to form a second layer. This increased weight and the cone head get the pattern deep quickly.

Often streamer patterns call for a body of gold or silver tinsel or one of the new synthetic materials like Flashabou or Krystal Flash. These materials are slippery and often slide back over the bend of the hook. As I discussed with the Patriot dry fly in Chapter 5, you can overcome this by leaving one strand behind at the bend and then bringing that over top of the other strands wound on the hook. Another way to cope with this problem is to rib the body with the same or similar tinsel. For example, with the Lady Ghost, tie in the oval tinsel first. Tie in this oval tinsel with the butt extending toward the eye a half-inch. Tie in the silver tinsel over top, and then rib the silver tinsel with the oval tinsel. This ribbing process will prevent the silver tinsel from slipping back over the bend.

One other problem many tiers encounter is getting the cheeks (if the pattern calls for these) on perfectly. To attain this, place a drop of epoxy on either side, then place the check feathers and let them dry. You can use the same technique to hold the wings in place. Other tiers have trouble getting the throat materials centered underneath. Try the same method George Harvey uses to get hackle underneath a wet-fly pattern. Take the material and tie it in at the right or the left side of the hook. Make about two or three turns of tying thread over the throat material. Next, slowly rotate the material underneath. This works much better if you have no other wing or cheek material in place.

We'll tie the Lady Ghost, Sparkle-Head Streamer, Golden Shiner, and Bead-Head Woolly Bugger.

THE BEAD-HEAD WOOLLY BUGGER

Poor patterns produce few lasting memories and good patterns generate some, but great patterns create endless memories. What great recollections the Bead-Head Woolly Bugger brings back every time I tie one. This large streamer-type pattern has saved me on several occasions when other dry flies and wet flies have failed.

There was that trip to the Little Colorado River in northern Arizona when Craig Josephson and I were warned by the river keeper that fishing had been terrible the past week. What a way to be greeted on a river! Besides, we had already fished an entire morning at the X-Diamond Ranch and never caught one trout. I didn't look forward to the next two days we had scheduled to fish at the ranch.

In desperation, I tied on a large Bead-Head Woolly Bugger—maybe this would work. It suddenly happened in the early afternoon—I landed a heavy trout. Soon I hooked a second heavy rainbow—then another. I yelled downriver to Craig to try a Bead-Head Woolly Bugger. He yelled back that he didn't have any with him, so I hurried down and handed him one. Within seconds, and on the first or second cast, Craig hooked a huge rainbow that he had trouble getting into his small, wooden net. That fantastic action continued well into the afternoon and until we both lost our last Woolly Buggers on frayed tippet material.

That same Woolly Bugger pattern has saved many opening days in Pennsylvania and New York.

Tie some of the patterns with lead weight added to the bodies before you tie them. Also try the reverse tying method for the ribbing. This technique is certainly not new, but it will strengthen the body considerably. Also tie some of these patterns with light gray bodies. As I said earlier, that color copies the common fish-fly larvae found in many streams across the country.

Dressing: Bead-Head Woolly Bugger
Hook: Mustad 79580, Size 10.
Bead: Copper.
Thread: Black 6/0.
Tail: A small bunch of black marabou and Flashabou.
Body: Three peacock herls or medium-dark olive chenille, ribbed with
    gold wire and palmered with a black saddle hackle.

1. Add the copper bead. Follow the directions for placing the bead on the hook in the tying directions for the Golden Shiner.
2. Optional: Add about twenty wraps of .010- or .015-inch lead wire to the body by wrapping from the rear toward the eye of the hook.

3. Take a small bunch (about twelve barbules) of black marabou and tie in for the tail. Make the tail about two-thirds the length of the shank of the hook. Also tie in about six pieces of silver Flashabou as part of the tail.

4. In front of the tail, tie in the three peacock herls or dark olive chenille, a long black saddle hackle, and a six-inch piece of gold wire. Wrap the peacock in your normal method up to the eye and tie off. Make certain you have the tying thread at the eye at this point.

5. *Next, take the gold wire and rib the peacock in the opposite direction. As you face the rear of the fly and look toward the eye, you previously wrapped the peacock from right to left. Rib the gold wire in the opposite direction.* **Ribbing in this manner prevents the fragile peacock from breaking.** *Tie in at the eye.*

6. Next, take the saddle hackle and palmer the body up to the eye. You should make five to seven wraps with the hackle.

7. Tie off and *cement. I cover the bead with at least two coats of clear nail polish. Let one coat dry and then apply a second coat.* **This helps prevent the bead from discoloring.**

THE LADY GHOST

I've mentioned before that I keep a short list of favorite patterns. I use these when no hatch appears on the water. These flies have worked for me for more than two decades. Currently my list of favorites includes the Green Weenie, Bead-Head Woolly Bugger, Bead-Head Pheasant-Tail Nymph, Glo Bug, Zebra Midge, Bead-Head Tan Caddis, I'm Not Sure, Bead-Head Olive Caddis, and Lady Ghost. Of all of these, the only one that has been on my favorites list for more than a decade is the Lady Ghost. This streamer has stood the test of time. No, I normally don't use the pattern in midsummer, but it has proven itself a productive pattern early in the season and on any occasion when you encounter high water.

The Lady Ghost has saved more than one opening day for me. I often resort to this pattern if the streams of spring are slightly off-color or a bit high. Let me explain. I still get excited about the first day of the trout season. After spending sixty of those opening days on one of many stocked streams, you'd think I'd lose my edge for them. But I don't, and I never will. Opening day signals a new beginning—a new season—a new life—a time to again spend enjoyable days outdoors. Some even have an added benefit, like hatches of hendricksons and pods of rising trout. I'll never forget one mid-April day when trout rose to mayflies for an entire afternoon. You know the format by now: Anglers who saw the trout rising tossed spinners, eggs, worms, cheese, and other baits at these risers, but they caught no fish.

I've also had my share of unsavory first days that I'd like to forget. Some were cold, overcast, and snowy, and with many others I've had heavy rains. The majority of opening days, and for that matter the first couple of weeks, often present cool water and high, off-color conditions. Using one pattern—the Lady Ghost—saved me more than once on some of those early-season trips. I'll never forget that mid-April day when I arrived at the stream late. Anglers had already begun fishing and I couldn't find an open area. I hiked downstream about a half-mile and found a pool and riffle that held no anglers. Surely, I thought, no one had planted any trout there or else there would have been other anglers. With the high and slightly off-color water, I decided to tie on a Lady Ghost and began casting in the riffle at the head of the pool. On the very first cast I felt a bump. On the second cast I hooked a trout almost fifteen inches long. Not bad—maybe even a good omen for the day and the season to come. Ten more trout quickly sucked in that Lady Ghost before I took a break.

But the Lady Ghost can save the day at times other than early spring. It happened in 1972. I discovered that the Little Juniata River held a good number of trout. That was long before other anglers found out how good this river really was. This river had just returned from a long bout with pollution and it was teeming with trout. I invited a group from the local Spring Creek Chapter of Trout Unlimited to fish the stream one evening. You guessed it—a heavy rainstorm pushed the river a foot or two above normal. The group met near Barree and we tried to decide what to do. Should we fish? The water was high but only slightly off-color. We decided to stay and I tied on a Lady Ghost streamer. That pattern caught three trout under those lousy conditions that evening.

As with most patterns I've used over a long period of time, I've changed it a bit here and there to where it is today. I've added a few pieces of Flashabou on top of the wing and to the tail to give some shine to the pattern. Adding this shiny material seems to make the Lady Ghost work even better.

Many classic streamer patterns call for jungle cock for the cheeks. Jungle cock is extremely rare, and when you can find it it's expensive. Many years ago I began adding pheasant body feathers (maroon-brown feathers with a black center top) for the cheek of the Lady Ghost. These are easy to obtain and work well. Strip them down to get the effect of the jungle cock.

Try the Lady Ghost. I feel you will find this old standby a perfect fit for those frustrating early-season trips and other inclement fishing days. Add Mirage Flashabou to the wing and tail, use pheasant body feathers for the cheeks, and you too will see a highly productive old streamer pattern with some new trimmings.

Dressing: Lady Ghost

Hook: Streamer hook, Size 10 or 12.

Thread: Black.

Tail: Mirage Flashabou.

Body: Mylar or flat tinsel, ribbed with oval tinsel.

Cheek: Dark maroon pheasant neck feather (with a black center tip).

Throat: White bucktail, yellow bucktail, peacock herls, and a few strands of Mirage Flashabou (tie in the white bucktail first).

Wing: Four golden badger hackles.

1. Tie in the black thread and wind back to the bend of the hook. *Tie in about a dozen Mirage Flashabou strands as a short tail. Have them extend out over the bend of the hook about one-quarter inch.* Tie in the flat and oval silver tinsel just in front of the tail. *Tie in the oval tinsel first and have the butt extend toward the eye a half-inch. Tie in the silver tinsel over top and then rib the silver tinsel with the oval tinsel.* **This ribbing process will prevent the silver tinsel from slipping back over the bend.**

2. Wrap the tinsel forward about three-quarters of the way up the shank and rib it with the oval tinsel. Tie both off.

3. Now add about six white bucktail, six yellow bucktail, and six peacock-herl fibers. Add Flashabou (six strands) underneath the other three. These four throat materials should extend a half-inch beyond the bend of the hook.

4. Add the four badger hackles on top. *These should also extend beyond the bend about a half-inch. Make certain that there are two hackles on either side. The shiny sides of all should face outward. On the right side have two hackles and on the left side two hackles. Have the dull sections of the inner two face each other. Wet the hackles to make them easier to form. Place a drop of epoxy on either side of the hook where you'll tie the wings, position the hackle, and let dry. Make a few wraps of tying thread over the butt sections of the hackle stems.*

5. *Place a drop of epoxy on either side of the cheek area where you want to place the pheasant feathers.* Strip the two feathers so you have the black center and a few brown outer fibers. Leave some of the stem so you can wind the tying thread over it later. *Position the feather until you're satisfied with the placement.* After the epoxy has dried, make a few turns with the tying thread to secure.

6. *Whip-finish in this manner: Take the end of a ballpoint pen, make three turns of the thread coming from the fly around the end of the pen (the hole where the ballpoint comes through), move the thread that is wrapped around the pen up to the eye of the hook, slide off and over the eye, and pull tight. You now have a whip-finish of sorts.*

7. Liberally apply epoxy on the head (see Golden Shiner).

THE SPARKLE-HEAD STREAMER

It rained for two days. The waters of the Deschutes River in central Oregon flowed high and a bit off-color. I came to this spectacular part of Oregon to fish the pale morning dun and salmon fly hatches. The giant down-wing salmon fly in late May can create some fantastic fishing opportunities, but not this day. What to do? I tied on a large new pattern that I had just developed called the Sparkle-Head Streamer. With its bright outer sheen, I felt trout might better be able to detect the pattern in the high, cloudy water.

I vividly remembered fishing the same run on the Deschutes just a couple of years earlier when the *Pteronarcys* stonefly crawled out of the water and appeared as a huge adult stonefly called the salmon fly. One rainbow after another had hit my large black nymph that day but no stonefly hatch appeared.

The waters ran high as I made my first casts with the Sparkle-Head Streamer. It didn't take long to determine the merits of this new pattern. The bead helped keep the pattern deep and the bright Flashabou attracted trout. That morning more than a dozen fish struck that new streamer.

When you tie this pattern, remember to place the bead near the bend and tie in the Flashabou. Have the Flashabou extend out over the eye and then slip the bead up to the eye. Make certain you have some of the Flashabou on the top, sides, and the bottom.

Try the Sparkle-Head Streamer, especially on those days when the waters you're fishing are high and off-color.

Dressing: Sparkle-Head Streamer
Hook: Streamer hook, Size 10 or 12.
Bead: Brass.
Thread: Black.
Tail: Mirage Flashabou.
Body: Oval tinsel.
Wing: Gray ostrich with Flashabou on top.

1. Slide on the bead and keep it at the bend of the hook. Make certain that you have a bead with a hole large enough to slide over the thread and Flashabou tips. Wrap the tying thread in at the eye of the hook.

2. *Tie in two dozen or more five-inch pieces of Flashabou at the hook eye and have them extend out over the eye. Make certain most are on the sides and bottom.* To get them on the bottom, first tie them on one side and then twist them underneath by moving them where they are tied in. Make a whip-finish, cut off the tying thread, and lacquer. Slip the bead up to the eye over the thread and the butts of the Flashabou. Wind the thread again, this time behind the bead, and wind the thread back to the bend of the hook.

3. Tie in about ten strands of Flashabou for the tail.

4. Tie in the oval tinsel and wind forward to the eye. Leave room for the wing.

5. Tie in about a half-dozen gray ostrich herls and place a half-dozen pieces of Flashabou on top.

6. *Now bring the Flashabou extending out over the eye back over the bead and tie off just in front of the wing and just behind the bead.*
7. Whip-finish and apply epoxy liberally to the head and bead.

THE GOLDEN SHINER

Talk about patterns that work on almost any trout stream in the world—the Golden Shiner has to be one of them. John Rohmer, an innovative fly tier, fly-shop owner, and distributor of fly-tying materials from Tempe, Arizona, first developed this particular pattern. John co-authored another popular book, *Arizona Trout Streams and Their Hatches*. Through his shop, John markets Semi Seal, the material I suggest for the belly. I recommend that you try this material for the body. Another southwestern angler, Chip Hidinger of Mesa, Arizona, showed me how to tie this streamer. Chip has tied flies for only about a half-dozen years, but I consider him one of the finest tiers I've seen. Chip has possibly accumulated almost as much fly-tying material in those few years as I have in more than fifty years of tying.

Chip has found that the Golden Shiner works equally well for smallmouth bass and lunker trout. Why is the Golden Shiner so productive? With the cone head and double lead weight it sinks rapidly. With the Variant rabbit strip on top and amber Semi Seal for the belly, it is lifelike and pulsating. It takes a bit of tying to get all the pieces in place but it's well worth the time. Besides, you'll learn several new techniques when you tie this pattern. You'll learn how to double up on the weighted body, use epoxy to hold the eyes in place, place large beads on hooks, and tease body material to make it fuller and more lifelike.

After you place the epoxy on the head, allow the pattern to dry thoroughly. Chip uses a rotary dryer that he built. This small drying motor rotates slowly—about five times a minute. You can find one of these motors at most electric supply houses. Cabela's also offers a rod turner that works great. Chip made a chuck out of two-inch PVC pipe.

This productive pattern evolved in the Southwest, but it works nationwide.

Dressing: Golden Shiner

Hook: Daiichi 2220, Size 10 to 14.

Thread: Tan 6/0.

Tail: Amber Semi Seal with part of the rabbit on top.

Body: Underbelly of amber Semi Seal with a strip of Variant rabbit on top and a ribbing of copper wire.

Head: A cone head in front and a red glass bead with a silver insert behind, and two eyes glued on with epoxy.

1. *Place the hook upside down in the vise. Have the point pointing directly up.* **This makes placing the bead on the hook much easier.** Place the cone head through the point. Next place the red glass bead through the point.

2. Place the hook in the vise upright and make six wraps of .025-inch lead wire from back to front and just in front of the eye. Now wind the wire back over itself. **This adds weight to the pattern and builds up the area just behind the eye of the hook.**

3. Move the tying thread to the bend of the hook and tie in a small bunch of amber Semi Seal for the tail.

4. In front of the tail tie in a six-inch piece of copper wire.

5. Make a dubbing loop and dub a five-inch piece of thread with the Semi Seal and wind to the eye.

6. Take a three-inch piece of a Variant rabbit strip, cut to shape (you want this approximately one-quarter inch wide) and tie in just behind

the eye of the hook. Make certain the strip extends out past the bend about one-third the length of the hook shank. Moisten the strip and stroke the hair upward (just as you do with a rooster hackle when you're preparing to make a wing on a streamer).

7. Rib the rabbit strip about four or five times with the copper wire that was left at the rear of the hook. Tie off the wire just behind the eye. Tie the thread off.

8. *Take a very small piece of Velcro, place some superglue on it, and attach it to a chopstick.* **Use it to tease the body hair of nymphs, streamers, and wet flies.** *Tease out the amber Semi Seal to form a fuller body. Trim a bit of the body after you tease it.*

9. Now form the head. First, place the eyes on the red bead. Next, mix the five-minute epoxy. Mix the two parts of the epoxy (about the size of a dime) thoroughly, and place small amounts around the eyes to keep them in place permanently and until you have the head built. **Cover the cone completely to prevent discoloration later.** Then place the finished fly on a dryer.

These four patterns are extremely productive. Try the Sparkle-Head Streamer and use the eleven new techniques listed in this chapter.

10

Stimulator Type Patterns

TECHNIQUES YOU WILL LEARN IN THIS CHAPTER

1. Tying a double tail to give the pattern more stability and to make it float better (Laid Back Hex, step 2)
2. How to make a large down-wing lie lower (nearer the body) (Laid Back Hex, steps 8 and 9, and Convertible, step 4)

Stimulator patterns—no way would I ever use one of those unusual patterns. That's how I felt about these weird flies for several years. In spite

of my trepidation, Stimulators, created by Randall Kaufmann, have become popular in the past decade. Anglers have found them successful in a variety of situations.

When should you use one of these down-wing patterns? Use them when copying down-wings like the stonefly or caddisfly, but also try them when copying some of the larger drake hatches. Hatches like the Hex in the Midwest and the green drake of the North are especially well copied by Stimulator-like patterns. I'm convinced they work well for some of the larger drake hatches because they suggest an emerger to the trout.

FISHING THE STIMULATOR

I said that I had nothing but disdain for Stimulators; that is until I traveled to Labrador in search of huge brook trout. On the Minipi River, Stimulators reigned supreme. Just ask Steve McDonald, of southeast Pennsylvania how well we did fishing Stimulators on the Minipi. These large flies worked especially well in Labrador when we fished them on top or tugged them just under the surface. Five- to eight-pound brook trout hit the patterns when a hatch of natural green drakes appeared.

Try using them when you encounter a *Pteronarcys* hatch in the East or West. These large stoneflies are common from late May until early July. You'll see much more concentrated hatches in the West, but some of the larger rivers of the Northeast, like the Delaware River, hold tremendous numbers of this huge stonefly. In the West the hatch is called the salmon fly, and here a Stimulator with a bright orange body works well.

TYING STIMULATOR TYPE PATTERNS

When you work with huge down-wings, you'll find an inherent problem keeping them low; the wings tend to stay high. If you follow one of my two suggestions when you tie the Laid Back Hex and the Convertible, you'll have much less difficulty accomplishing this.

Another problem with large patterns is difficulty keeping them floating. Adding hackle to these patterns helps them float much better.

THE LAID BACK HEX

This refined version of the Stimulator (or maybe the Stimulator is a version of the Laid Back Hex) worked well in Labrador. Rusty Gates, a well-known fly fisher and fly-shop owner on the AuSable River in Michigan, first tied this pattern twenty years ago.

Rusty ties other productive patterns that work well during the Hex hatch. One of these Hex patterns has a white hair wing placed at an angle (almost down-wing) and the same tail configuration as the Laid Back Hex. Rusty ties on a cream-olive body and a large dark brown hackle wound around the white hair post. It's a terrific pattern when the Hex hatch appears.

Rusty's Laid Back Hex is one of my favorite patterns. My son, Bryan, went out to Michigan recently to witness the Hex hatch and the related activity (see his account in *The Hatches Made Simple*). He found that the Laid Back Hex works well on the AuSable in late June, especially when that large hatch appears at night. Bryan gave me a couple of the Hex patterns, and I took them with me on my trip to Labrador to Cooper's Minipi Lodge. That fly, and a version of it called the Convertible (described later in this chapter), caught more trout than any other pattern that enjoyable week.

Tie the Laid Back Hex with body colors in olive, brown, cream, yellow, and gray. I feel certain that this pattern can represent many different hatches. Also try the other Hex pattern (with the white wings) I discussed earlier.

Dressing: Laid Back Hex
Hook: Mustad 94831, Size 6 to 16.
Thread: The same color as the body (in this case yellow). In addition, cut off a five-inch piece of tying thread that you'll use at the bend of the hook (or make the loop in your tying thread).
Tail: Two long pheasant tail fibers and a dozen shorter deer-hair fibers.
Body: Rusty Gates uses sparkle rug yarn or UNI yarn; you can use poly yarn in yellow, cream, olive, brown, or gray. On top will be the deer

hair brought from the tail and tied in at the wing. In the description below I'm using yellow poly.

Wing: Deer hair tied down-wing.

Hackle: Brown and grizzly tied in halfway up the shank, palmered to the wing, and cut off on the bottom.

1. Tie in the pheasant tail fibers. Make certain they're almost as long as the shank of the hook.

2. Tie in about a dozen deer-hair fibers at the bend of the hook. The fibers should be very short. Don't cut off the butts—you'll use them later. ***These tails will help float the heavy pattern.*** Leave a piece of yellow tying thread at the bend of the hook by making a loop in your tying thread, tying it off, and cutting one end at the shank.

3. Wind dubbed yellow material up the shank halfway to the eye.

4. Tie in a brown and a grizzly hackle where you've ended the back half of the body, then continue the yellow body up to the eye. Leave enough room for the wing.

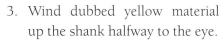

5. Palmer the two hackles (at the same time if you can) up the front half of the body. Cut off the bottom hackle fibers.

6. Move the hackle fibers on top to the right and left, or cut off the top hackle fibers and bring the butt section of the deer hair up and over the body and tie in just behind the eye. Clip off the excess.

7. Bring the loose piece of yellow tying thread at the bend of the hook and rib the deer hair to the eye. Be careful not to crimp down the palmered hackle.

8. Tie in, down-wing style, two dozen deer-hair fibers and clip off the butts to form a small head like that of the Muddler Minnow. *Make certain some of the deer hair is on either side to help the large pattern float. Place some cement at the head of the deer hair and hold down the wings with the loop of the hackle pliers until the cement sets. (Slide the loop of the pliers over the hook.)*

9. *A second method to keep the wing low: After you make plenty of wraps around the butt section of the wing, make several loose wraps ⅟₁₆ to ⅛ of an inch behind, then move back to where you originally tied off the butt.*

10. Optional: I sometimes add a brown hackle at this point—similar to the Stimulator—to make the pattern float higher.

11. Whip-finish.

Rusty cuts off the hackle fibers on the top and the bottom of the pattern to make it float more flush with the surface to suggest an emerging nymph. It worked for me in Labrador. Try this pattern for some of the more common and larger hatches, especially when the trout become highly selective.

THE CONVERTIBLE

Why is this pattern called the Convertible? First, it looks like a Stimulator and it copies many of the larger caddis, stoneflies, and yes, even some of the larger emerging mayflies and hoppers. But sink the pattern and it becomes a Muddler type pattern.

Does it produce when you use it to copy a large emerging mayfly drake? You bet it does! What a week in Labrador! A tremendous hatch and behemoth brook trout taking duns on the surface. They took the green drake of the North (*Hexagenia rigida*). I tied up a few simple patterns that had short deer-hair tails, twisted yellow bodies, and down-wing deer-hair wings with hackle in front. That first evening I used the Convertible I caught two trout by floating the pattern on the surface. Trout began taking emergers and I tugged the pattern underneath the surface. That wet fly took two more heavy brook trout.

Add some weight to the tippet and you have a great Muddler type pattern. The Convertible is a must for your arsenal of flies.

Dressing: The Convertible
Hook: Mustad 94831, Size 6 to 16.
Thread: Yellow 6/0.
Tail: Short deer hair.
Body: Yellow poly yarn.
Wings: Deer hair tied down-wing.
Hackle: Cree.

1. Tie in a dozen deer hairs for the tail. Make them about one-third the length of the hook shank.

2. Spin a five-inch piece of poly yarn about twenty times with a hackle pliers or with your hand. Put the two ends of the twisted material together and you should see part of the material curl up. Extend the tip of the twisted poly yarn out over the body about a half-inch. Tie in the body above the point of the hook.

3. Dub some yellow poly the same color as the poly yarn and wind up the shank about three-quarters of the way.

4. Tie in a bunch of long deer hair about the size of a wooden matchstick, down-wing style. Let some of the deer hair lie on the right and left sides to help balance the pattern. Clip the butts. *Hold down the wings with a retractable clothespin or a hackle pliers, and put cement at the butts just above where they are tied in.* **This will make the long down-wing**

stay closer to the body. *Let the cement dry before doing the next step.*

5. Tie two cree hackles at the head and wing. Cover the head completely with the thread.

6. Clip off stray deer hair.

7. Whip-finish and cement.

You might detest these oversized patterns and think that they can only be used in the West. Tie some of them and use them when some of the larger mayflies, stoneflies, and caddisflies appear.

11

Now It's Your Turn

By now you've tried at least a few of the techniques that I've discussed. As I've indicated many times, I'm a lazy tier and I always look for more simplified, quicker, or easier ways to tie a fly. You should have found some shortcuts throughout the book that will make your tying easier.

Take, for instance, the methods of securing and dividing upright wings in Chapter 5. How about the method for preventing body materials from moving back over the bend of the hook? That's also found in Chapter 5. Or maybe you like to tie down-wings and you've found the Deer-Head Caddis to your liking. This pattern and the easy method of tying the head and wing have saved me on many trips. What about the method in Chapter 8 to prevent hackle from climbing up and over a post? That procedure has worked well for me for years. One of my favorites is twisting poly yarn and other materials to make lifelike, segmented bodies. You've learned these techniques in Chapters 6 and 8. Or maybe you like the Swimming Ephemera Nymph. It's truly a lifelike pattern.

There are those who would make you think that there is only one correct way to tie flies. But there is no one correct way of tying. Incorporate those tying methods and procedures that you feel most comfortable with and discard those you feel don't help.

I have been tying flies for more than fifty years and I've learned from many different fly tiers. What I've presented in this book are those tying procedures that make my tying even easier and quicker. Yes, a lot of these you might already use, but learning just a few shortcuts and tricks will cut down your tying time and make the whole process more accommodating.

YOUR OWN INNOVATIVE TECHNIQUES

Do you have some of your own innovative fly-tying techniques? If you've been tying for any period then I'm certain you have some. Let me know about some of yours. They might appear in the next edition of *101 Innovative Fly-Tying Techniques*.

Index